How To Memorize Super Complex Passwords Containing Numbers, Alphabets And Special Characters Using A Variety Of Peg Systems

By

Emmanuel Q.-M. Bruce-Adjei

Table of Contents

Introduction

Passwords are required for online accounts at various websites, social media accounts, online banking accounts, access to your email addresses, and for the protection of personal and confidential information in order to avoid unwelcomed and disastrous data breaches and data losses. Passwords must be strong and secure. Strong and secure passwords should be long, at least ten characters, and must contain numbers, alphabets and special characters, but should not contain personal or business addresses, names of popular landmarks, dictionary names, names of favorite cars, names of pets, birthdays, bible verses, names of movie stars, short dialogs in movies, proverbs, and other common names. Even if you are using a password manager for all your passwords, you will still need a strong and secure password to access the other passwords on your password manager.

However strong a password is, if it is written down somewhere, and there is unauthorized access to it, it can be fatal and catastrophic. We are therefore going to learn how to use peg systems based on mnemonics to process passwords. The peg system codes the numbers, alphabets and special characters into peg words. The peg words are then used to form a sequence of sentences in order to chain or link the peg words sequentially and coherently together. If you memorize the sentences in the correct order, you can be able to sequentially and coherently extract the peg words and then decode them into the original characters in order to obtain the original passwords.

The peg systems we will use are the following:

- Number Rhyme Peg System

- Number Shape Peg System
- Phonetic Number Peg System
- Number-Object Peg System
- Alphabet Rhyme Peg System
- Special Character Rhyme Peg System

This book is unique in that lots and lots of passwords had been generated in it. There are innumerable examples and practice exercises. Some of the generated passwords are really indubitably and indisputably, aesthetically elegant, and you may be comprehensibly tempted to use them as they are. You are, however, advised not to use any of the passwords generated in this book without modifying it with your own numbers, alphabets and special characters and/or jumbling the characters around to change it. Never use any password in this book as it is.

You can individually memorize the relevant peg words and some examples already given in this book, and try and see whether you can recall the original passwords. Use this as a test run before working through the practice exercises. You can also use some of the numerous passwords generated in this book to test the ability of your friends and peers to master these memorization techniques.

Have fun!

Chapter 1

Number Rhyme Peg System

In this system, the numbers are associated with words which rhyme or nearly rhyme with them. However, finding such rhymes or near-rhymes for the numbers is a daunting task. However, you can use any words you think closely rhyme with the numbers.

Here are some rhymes and near-rhymes for the numbers zero to twenty:

Table 1.1   Numbers and Peg Words

Number	Peg Word
0	Hero
1	Hun
2	Shoe
3	Tree
4	Door
5	Hive
6	Hicks
7	Heaven
8	Gate
9	Mine
10	Hen
11	Leaven
12	Shelf
13	Tithing
14	Farthing
15	Christine
16	Sistine

17	Séverine
18	Aden
19	Nicene
20	Twinkle

Learning Procedure

1. You memorize the numbers and their associated peg words. Memorize them very well through repetition and reinforcement because you will always have to remember them in order to recall the passwords.
2. You find the peg words for the numbers in the password and arrange them in the order in which they appear in the password.
3. You construct sentences with the peg words in order to chain or link them sequentially and coherently together. The more outrageous a sentence is, the easier it is for you to remember it.
4. You memorize the sentences in order to get the correct positions of the peg words in the sentences with absolute ease.
5. You will then be able to remember the password if you remember the numbers and their associated peg words.

How to Memorize the Sentences Constructed with the Peg Words

You will use repetition and reinforcement to learn these sentences.

1. Read the sentences inaudibly five or ten times.
2. Read the sentences audibly five or ten times.
3. Write down the sentences five or ten times.

Please continue this process till you can easily remember the sentences.

Please note that we have used the uppercase for initial letters of specific words or specific words in the groups of words in the sentences constructed in this book and bolded them only for emphasis and clarity. We crave your indulgence if you are unhappy that this may be an irremissible infraction of the rules of grammar.

1.1 Number Rhyme Examples

Example 1:   Password Length = 4 characters
Password: 8758
Peg Words: 8-7-5-8

first Gate	Heaven
Hive	second Gate

Sentence(s):
The first **Gate** to **Heaven** faced the **Hive** which was behind the second **Gate**.

Example 2:   Password Length = 5 characters
Password: 29413
Peg Words: 2-9-4-13

Shoe	Mine
Door	Tithing

Sentence(s):
The **Shoe** was found in the **Mine** which was not far from the **Door** leading to the **Tithing** room.

Example 3:   Password Length = 6 characters
Password: 961572
Peg Words: 9-6-15-7-2

Mine	Hicks
Christine	Heaven
Shoe	

Sentence(s):

The **Mine** which belonged to the **Hicks** was sold to **Christine** who went to **Heaven** with only one **Shoe**.

Example 4: Password Length = 7 characters
Password: 5686317
Peg Words: 5-6-8-6-3-17

Hive	first Hicks
Gate	second Hicks
Tree	Séverine

Sentence(s):

The **Hive** of the first group of **Hicks** was close to the **Gate** of the garden of the second group of **Hicks** where a **Tree** had been planted by **Séverine**.

Example 5: Password Length = 8 characters
Password: 34744060
Peg Words: 3-4-7-4-4-0-6-0

Tree	first Door
Heaven	second Door
third Door	first Hero
Hicks	second Hero

Sentence(s):

The **Tree** was in front of the first **Door** to the main hall in **Heaven**, the second **Door**, and the third **Door** led to the chambers of the first **Hero** where the **Hicks** and the second **Hero** were relaxing on couches.

Example 6: Password Length = 9 characters
Password: 491429385
Peg Words: 4-9-14-2-9-3-8-5

Door	first Mine

Farthing	Shoe
second Mine	Tree
Gate	Hive

Sentence(s):

The **Door** lock of the storage cabinet in the first **Mine** cost a **Farthing** more than the **Shoe**, and the opening to the second **Mine** was facing the **Tree**, which was in the garden and close to the **Gate**, which led to the **Hive**.

Example 7:   Password Length = 10 characters
Password: 7844626652
Peg Words: 7-8-4-4-6-2-6-6-5-2

Heaven	Gate
first Door	second Door
first Hicks	first Shoe
second Hicks	third Hicks
Hive	second Shoe

Sentence(s):

He went to **Heaven** through a **Gate** which led through the first **Door** and the second **Door** to the throne room, where the first group of **Hicks** was guarding the first **Shoe**, and the second group of **Hicks** and the third group of **Hicks** had put the **Hive** in front of the second **Shoe** to hide it.

Example 8:   Password Length = 11 characters
Password: 99046029027
Peg Words: 9-9-0-4-6-0-2-9-0-2-7

first Mine	second Mine
first Hero	Door
Hicks	second Hero
first Shoe	third Mine
third Hero	second Shoe

Heaven

Sentence(s):

The first **Mine** and the second **Mine** belonged to the first **Hero**, the main **Door** of whose mansion was damaged by the **Hicks**, and the second **Hero** took the first **Shoe** to the third **Mine** where the third **Hero** was keeping the second **Shoe** before he went to **Heaven**.

Example 9:   Password Length = 12 characters
Password: 844475616022
Peg Words: 8-4-4-4-7-5-6-16-0-2-2

Gate	first Door
second Door	third Door
Heaven	Hive
Hicks	Sistine
Hero	first Shoe
second Shoe	

Sentence(s):

The main **Gate**, the first **Door**, second **Door** and third **Door** all led to **Heaven** where the **Hive** belonging to the **Hicks**, who were blessed in the **Sistine** Chapel, was being kept, and the **Hero** took the first **Shoe** and the second **Shoe** and threw them away.

Example 10:   Password Length = 13 characters
Password: 7861059084157
Peg Words: 7-8-6-10-5-9-0-8-4-15-7

first Heaven	first Gate
Hicks	Hen
Hive	Mine
Hero	second Gate
Door	Christine
second Heaven	

Sentence(s):

The first **Heaven** had the first **Gate** through which the **Hicks** took the **Hen** and the **Hive** to the **Mine**, and the **Hero** passed through the second **Gate** and the **Door** of the living room of **Christine** and went to the second **Heaven**.

Example 11:   Password Length = 14 characters
Password: 40118518749452
Peg Words: 4-0-11-8-5-18-7-4-9-4-5-2

first Door	Hero
Leaven	Gate
first Hive	Aden
Heaven	second Door
Mine	third Door
second Hive	Shoe

Sentence(s):

He went through the first **Door** and saw the **Hero**, who showed him where the **Leaven** was before passing through the **Gate** and going straight to the first **Hive** hanging in the barn, he claimed that **Aden** was a gateway to **Heaven** and then passed through the second **Door** towards the **Mine** before turning right to the third **Door** and moving towards the second **Hive** and the **Shoe**.

Example 12:   Password Length = 15 characters
Password: 870126452072893
Peg Words: 8-7-0-12-6-4-5-20-7-2-8-9-3

first Gate	first Heaven
Hero	Shelf
Hicks	Door
Hive	Twinkle
second Heaven	Shoe
second Gate	Mine

Tree

Sentence(s):

At the first **Gate** to the first **Heaven**, the **Hero** was sitting on the **Shelf** looking at the **Hicks**, who rushed through the **Door** with the **Hive** in the **Twinkle** of an eye, and in the second **Heaven**, the **Shoe** was placed before the second **Gate** which led to the **Mine** and the **Tree**.

Example 13: Password Length = 16 characters
Password: 1967618357581621
Peg Words: 19-6-7-6-18-3-5-7-5-8-16-2-1

Nicene	first Hicks
first Heaven	second Hicks
Aden	Tree
first Hive	second Heaven
second Hive	Gate
Sistine	Shoe
Hun	

Sentence(s):

The **Nicene** Creed was read to the first group of **Hicks** in the first **Heaven** whilst the second group of **Hicks** went to **Aden** to look at the **Tree** with the first **Hive**, and in the second **Heaven**, the second **Hive** was close to the main **Gate** of the courtyard of the **Sistine** Chapel, where the **Shoe** of the **Hun** had been placed in front of the altar.

Example 14: Password Length = 17 characters
Password: 01134342699440908
Peg Words: 0-11-3-4-3-4-2-6-9-9-4-4-0-9-0-8

first Hero	Leaven
first Tree	first Door
second Tree	second Door

Shoe	Hicks
first Mine	second Mine
third Door	fourth Door
second Hero	third Mine
third Hero	Gate

Sentence(s):

The first **Hero** put some **Leaven** in the dough and went to the first **Tree** through the first **Door** and then to the second **Tree** through the second **Door** and threw the **Shoe** at the **Hicks.**, and the first **Mine** and the second **Mine** could be reached through the third **Door** and fourth **Door** where the second **Hero** who owned the third **Mine** was talking to the third **Hero** at the **Gate**.

Example 15: Password Length = 18 characters
Password: 085195401232450641
Peg Words: 0-8-5-19-5-4-0-12-3-2-4-5-0-6-4-1

first Hero	Gate
first Hive	Nicene
second Hive	first Door
second Hero	Shelf
Tree	Shoe
second Door	third Hive
third Hero	Hicks
third Hero	Hun

Sentence(s):

The first **Hero** went through the **Gate** with the first **Hive** without saying the **Nicene** Creed, and took the second **Hive** and passed through the first **Door** and gave it to the second **Hero** who put it on the **Shelf** under the **Tree**, he then took the **Shoe**, went through the second **Door**, took the third **Hive** and gave it to the third **Hero** who gave it to the **Hicks** who run through the third **Door** and gave it to the **Hun**.

Example 16:   Password Length = 19 characters
Password: 6532206617245092827
Peg Words: 6-5-3-2-20-6-6-17-2-4-5-0-9-2-8-2-7

first Hicks	first Hive
Tree	first Shoe
Twinkle	second Hicks
third Hicks	Séverine
second Shoe	Door
second Hive	Hero
Mine	third Shoe
Gate	fourth Shoe
Heaven	

Sentence(s):

The first group of **Hicks** took the first **Hive** from the **Tree** and the first **Shoe** in the twinkle of an eye, and the second group of **Hicks** and the third group of **Hicks**, who said that **Séverine** had taken the second **Shoe,** passed through the **Door**, and gave them to the **Hero** who went to the **Mine** and took the third **Shoe,** passed through the **Gate**, and then took the fourth **Shoe** and went to **Heaven**.

Example 17:   Password Length = 20 characters
Password: 58860320478033881180
Peg Words: 5-8-8-6-0-3-20-4-7-8-0-3-3-8-8-11-8-0

Hive	first Gate
second Gate	Hicks
first Hero	first Tree
Twinkle	Door
Heaven	third Gate
second Hero	second Tree
third Tree	fourth Gate

| fifth Gate | Leaven |
| sixth Gate | third Hero |

Sentence(s):

The man took the **Hive** and went through the first **Gate** and the second **Gate** and gave it to the **Hicks**, who also gave it to the first **Hero**, standing in front of the first **Tree** with a **Twinkle** in his eye, expecting to pass through the **Door** to **Heaven**, and the third **Gate** was close to where the second **Hero** was standing and looking at the second **Tree** and the third **Tree** before passing through the fourth **Gate** and fifth **Gate**, and taking the **Leaven** through the sixth **Gate** and giving it to the third **Hero** for the preparation of the bread.

Example 18:   Password Length = 21 characters
Password: 80200799470490817635
Peg Words: 8-0-20-0-7-9-9-9-4-7-0-4-9-0-8-17-6-3-5

first Gate	first Hero
Twinkle	second Hero
first Heaven	first Mine
second Mine	third Mine
first Door	second Heaven
third Hero	second Door
fourth Mine	fourth Hero
second Gate	Séverine
Hicks	Tree
Hive	

Sentence(s):

The first **Gate** was where the first **Hero** passed in the **Twinkle** of an eye and met the second **Hero,** who went to the first **Heaven**, and then passed through the first **Mine**, the second **Mine** and the third **Mine** and then the first **Door** to the second **Heaven**, and the third **Hero** passed through the second **Door** and the fourth **Mine** to the fourth **Hero** and together they went through the second **Gate** and saw **Séverine** arguing with the **Hicks** under the **Tree**, from which the **Hive** was hanging.

Example 19:   Password Length = 22 characters
Password: 3710110168097289759684
Peg Words: 3-7-10-11-0-16-8-0-9-7-2-8-9-7-5-9-6-8-4

Tree	first Heaven
Hen	Leaven
first Hero	Sistine
first Gate	second Hero
first Mine	second Heaven
Shoe	second Gate
second Mine	third Heaven
Hive	third Mine
Hicks	third Gate
Door	

Sentence(s):
The **Tree** in front of the first **Heaven** was the roosting place of the **Hen**, and the **Leaven** was taken by the first **Hero** to the **Sistine** Chapel through the first **Gate**, where the second **Hero** had passed the first **Mine** to enter the second **Heaven**.

The **Shoe** was taken through the second **Gate** and the second **Mine** to the third **Heaven**, and the **Hive** was taken through the third **Mine** to the **Hicks**, who had entered through the third **Gate** and the main **Door**.

Example 20:   Password Length = 23 characters
Password: 75171619255742547733537
Peg Words: 7-5-17-16-19-2-5-5-7-4-2-5-4-7-7-3-3-5-3-7

first Heaven	first Hive
Séverine	Sistine

Nicene	first Shoe
second Hive	third Hive
second Heaven	first Door
second Shoe	fourth Hive
second Door	third Heaven
fourth Heaven	first Tree
second Tree	fifth Hive
third Tree	fifth Heaven

Sentence(s):

Into the first **Heaven** was the first **Hive** that **Séverine** took from the **Sistine** Chapel after saying the **Nicene** Creed, and the first **Shoe**, the second **Hive** and the third **Hive** were taken to the second **Heaven** through the first **Door**.

He took the second **Shoe** and the fourth **Hive**, and then passed through the second **Door** and sent them to the third **Heaven** and the fourth **Heaven**, and he came to the first **Tree**, the second **Tree**, the fourth **Hive** and the third **Tree** before going to the fifth **Heaven**.

Example 21: Password Length = 24 characters

Password: 143462238060155256526586

Peg Words: 14-3-4-6-2-2-3-8-0-6-0-15-5-2-5-6-5-2-6-5-8-6

Farthing	first Tree
Door	first Hicks
first Shoe	second Shoe
second Tree	first Gate
first Hero	second Hicks
second Hero	Christine
first Hive	third Shoe
second Hive	third Hicks
third Hive	fourth Shoe

fourth Hicks	fourth Hive
second Gate	fifth Hicks

Sentence(s):

A **Farthing** was found under the first **Tree** opposite the **Door** through which the first group of **Hicks** took the first **Shoe** and the second **Shoe**, which were hanging from the second **Tree** near the first **Gate**, and where the first **Hero**, the second group of **Hicks** and second **Hero** were railing at **Christine**.

The first **Hive**, the third **Shoe** and the second **Hive** were given to the third group of **Hicks** and the third **Hive** and fourth **Shoe** were given to the fourth group of **Hicks**, who also took the fourth **Hive**, passed through the second **Gate** and gave it to the fifth group of **Hicks**.

Example 22:   Password Length = 25 characters
Password: 2979185296416454060136537
Peg Words: 2-9-7-9-18-5-2-9-6-4-16-4-5-4-0-6-0-13-6-5-3-7

first Shoe	first Mine
first Heaven	second Mine
Aden	first Hive
second Shoe	third Mine
first Hicks	first Door
Sistine	second Door
second Hive	third Door
first Hero	second Hicks
second Hero	Tithing
third Hicks	third Hive
Tree	second Heaven

Sentence(s):

The first **Shoe**, which was taken from the first **Mine**, was sent to the first **Heaven** and the second **Mine** in **Aden** which had the first **Hive**, the second **Shoe** and the third **Mine**, which belonged to the first group of **Hicks**, who passed through the first **Door** of the **Sistine** Chapel, and then went to the second **Door** and then straight into courtyard.

The second **Hive** was taken through the third **Door** by the first **Hero** who gave it to the second group of **Hicks** who congratulated the second **Hero** for **Tithing**, but the third group of **Hicks** took the third **Hive** from the **Tree** and sent it to the second **Heaven**.

1.2   Number Rhyme Practice Exercises

Exercises 1:   Password Length = 4 characters
4401
4517
3570
3118
8885
5511
3368
3468
4379
4469

Exercises 2:   Password Length = 5 characters
96404
74815
17907
83967
81747
23254
21636
36905
95683
18275

Exercises 3:   Password Length = 6 characters

631731
191034
094154
158869
530787
578044
547422
184621
841435

Exercises 4:   Password Length = 7 characters

7934386
7794358
0379426
8072290
5770575
1948003
6037845
9762500
1376130
3511257

Exercises 5:   Password Length = 8 characters

64240414
40445250
56673935
51791237
10323098
81034152
45805682
79542679
38692946
60460281

Exercises 6:   Password Length = 9 characters
643183201
641623667
543036295
742278171
563649942
355492769
131137414
225179428
970336884
693903492

Exercises 7:   Password Length = 10 characters
5727884460
7048000304
0530588937
7585143541
3310087219
6206012103
4798949846
7507618528
6735092956
4437366804

Exercises 8:   Password Length = 11 characters
04759112974
51072748002
75869702877
97748123252
79431083541
14766028866
30124971756
17618712386
65135616734
92617699814

Exercises 9:   Password Length = 12 characters

426161293851
363554940374
937468376554
747174426473
489779135613
052936734713
596474882706
214459198590
359482661253
810639711822

Exercises 10:   Password Length = 13 characters

1388456941908
9448624673044
6253267280125
9241428423966
8357540011661
3444385410192
4904461178286
8757686795186
4393136196542
8930715442201

Exercises 11:   Password Length = 14 characters

48002490242524
28401200265691
96212511240392
81469280382706
01403654404701
02624291953243
21581247105183
01254474722819
50712318697337
86917185797294

Exercises 12:   Password Length = 15 characters

651147068390797
427399459600042
149407165147345
447679141958405
956226993752211
709014293703849
538696396867969
221445255705933
608000849794996
796545962663102

Exercises 13:   Password Length = 16 characters

6966626918883157
7891047463010052
3928525344260194
0612921183525026
4947627823142621
3567371445175552
2732551795821390
8223036525022950
7213782744561610
8767843890996542

Exercises 14:   Password Length = 17 characters

53057980332834684
31449537203625550
01661216980956553
37472991631327112
41955036614500630
67570737572599484
15344855073180570
67348462494186994
20113743345476280
28632517185203669

Exercises 15:   Password Length = 18 characters

386264990934811957
526204235274977616
768436548371752964
432970241237262372
497122068903492090
399669140749036390
451114194240651980
748288844436795359
852818704629478271
162865638354683012

Exercises 16:   Password Length = 19 characters

3589278382671170384
2001803661836244225
7350608026433096928
5651909509971230857
3710653106032012933
2048433202045127838
2127041691962794472
4440216643944925025
6126099660802047878
7849527311284827128

Exercises 17:   Password Length = 20 characters

47368055646025603972
93782463515188205516
10932993155991056445
48624833419861979583
30753822001461086408
63656783783732374677
22614583986449926059
57501902732618353668
09779429233363201200
57303415835018617078

Exercises 18:   Password Length = 21 characters

522544446187977625267
682300166107491373276
194739995102363217559
745690397484194289583
173407810351864153365
581906219661483303955
104921208572255125009
661561301943598232547
682917523506134385720
910105801739061744264

Exercises 19:   Password Length = 22 characters

3482330993167608394849
4276750665342868688079
9999005690616215196782
9427141842474198375446
9532878932713456372021
9040815212443205021023
6972435968383225579458
8008251579436673598677
7146927015473598256397
5976239204032029019168

Exercises 20:   Password Length = 23 characters

31088233124254294151779
75589931865577105531756
30335044784149305844252
45037855485644158382675
01006736987422105313829
74033374814392453698343
04025986669936217277364
59986194321974779001060
14384021358839061930602
83674969000097710935162

Exercises 21:   Password Length = 24 characters

633042346129628511515229
751638414677054407004685
724514334237772726349134
752492800946866284963322
410950057416913181335550
105950951183964362886740
390171577398597375779337
452682398947479280494045
805580442782199152820273
161849735805313243189739

Exercises 22:   Password Length = 25 characters

2021453722233339273478145
5156251677953919355143774
6196844034092269652933535
9491250094989627467587111
0683799060149556705059926
2511717393642466215241518
2110193330685283993252702
5833866038720642508508862
3070407356685120851738944
8066914117473104595752361

Chapter 2

Number Shape Peg System

The peg words we are going to use here physically resemble the digits or numbers. We have decided to utilize peg words for the numbers 0 to 10.

Here are therefore the peg words for the numbers from 0 to 10:

Table 2.1 Numbers and Peg Words

Number	Peg Words
0	Egg
1	Pen
2	Swan
3	Camel's Double Hump
4	Chair
5	Hook
6	Golf Club
7	Axe
8	Hourglass
9	Tadpole
10	Fork And Plate

Please note that we have used the uppercase for initial letters of specific words or specific words in the groups of words in the sentences constructed in this book and bolded them only for emphasis and clarity. We crave your indulgence if you are unhappy that this may be an irremissible infraction of the rules of grammar.

Learning Procedure

1. You memorize the numbers and their associated peg words. Memorize them very well through repetition and reinforcement because you will always have to remember them in order to recall the passwords.
2. You find the peg words for the numbers in the password and arrange them in the order in which they appear in the password.
3. You construct sentences with the peg words in order to chain or link them sequentially and coherently together. The more outrageous a sentence is, the easier it is for you to remember it.
4. You memorize the sentences in order to get the correct positions of the peg words in the sentences with absolute ease.
5. You will then be able to remember the password if you remember the numbers and their associated peg words.

How to Memorize the Sentences Constructed with the Peg Words

You will use repetition and reinforcement to learn these sentences.

1. Read the sentences inaudibly five or ten times.
2. Read the sentences audibly five or ten times.
3. Write down the sentences five or ten times.

Please continue this process till you can easily remember the sentences.

2.1 Number Shape Examples

Example 1:   Password Length = 4 characters
Password: 5698

Peg Words: 5-6-9-8

Hook	Golf Club
Tadpole	Hourglass

Sentence(s):

The **Hook** was holding the **Golf Club** on the wall and the **Tadpole** was wriggling on the **Hourglass**.

Example 2: Password Length = 5 characters

Password: 67130

Peg Words: 6-7-1-3-0

Golf Club	Axe
Pen	Camel's Double Hump
Egg	

Sentence(s):

He took the **Golf Club** and the **Axe**, he slashed the **Pen**, and hit the **Camel's Double Hump** and an **Egg** came out of it.

Example 3: Password Length = 6 characters

Password: 331249

Peg Words: 3-3-1-2-4-9

first Camel's Double Hump	second Camel's Double Hump
Pen	Swan
Chair	Tadpole

Sentence(s):

He pierced the first **Camel's Double Hump** and the second **Camel's Double Hump** with the **Pen** and looked at the **Swan** sitting on the **Chair** with a **Tadpole** in its beak.

Example 4: Password Length = 7 characters

Password: 1283027

Peg Words: 1-2-8-3-0-2-7

Pen	first Swan

Hourglass	Camel's Double Hump
Egg	second Swan
Axe	

Sentence(s):

The **Pen** was in the beak of the first **Swan**, the **Hourglass** was resting on the **Camel's Double Hump**, and the **Egg** was being incubated by the second **Swan** which was attached to the **Hook**.

Example 5: Password Length = 8 characters
Password: 23087130
Peg Words: 2-3-0-8-7-1-3-0

Swan	first Camel's Double Hump
first Egg	Hourglass
Axe	Pen
second Camel's Double Hump	second Egg

Sentence(s):

The **Swan** was sitting on the first **Camel's Double Hump** looking at the first **Egg** and the **Hourglass** on the ground where the **Axe** has cut the **Pen** into two pieces whilst the second **Camel's Double Hump** was carrying the second **Egg**.

Example 6: Password Length = 9 characters
Password: 671081536
Peg Words: 6-7-10-8-1-5-3-6

first Golf Club	Axe
Fork And Plate	Hourglass
Pen	Hook
Camel's Double Hump	second Golf Club

Sentence(s):

The first **Golf Club** hit the **Axe** after it had smashed the **Fork And Plate** and the **Hourglass,** and the **Pen** was hanging from the **Hook** attached to the **Camel's Double Hump**, and the second **Golf Club** was lying on the ground.

Example 7: Password Length = 10 characters
Password: 3784063822
Peg Words: 3-7-8-4-0-6-3-8-2-2

first Camel's Double Hump	Axe
first Hourglass	Chair
Egg	Golf Club
second Camel's Double Hump	second Hourglass
first Swan	second Swan

Sentence(s):

On the first **Camel's Double Hump**, lay the **Axe** for one hour as indicated by the first **Hourglass**, which was on the **Chair**, and the **Egg** was broken with the **Golf Club**, and the second **Camel's Double Hump** bore the second **Hourglass,** and the first **Swan** and the second **Swan** were standing on the shores of the lake.

Example 8: Password Length = 11 characters
Password: 13176047838
Peg Words: 1-3-1-7-6-0-4-7-8-3-8

first Pen	first Camel's Double Hump
second Pen	first Axe
Golf Club	Egg
Chair	second Axe
first Hourglass	second Camel's Double Hump
second Hourglass	

Sentence(s):

The first **Pen** was on the first **Camel's Double Hump**, the second **Pen** was cut with the first **Axe** and the **Golf Club** was used to hit the **Egg** on the **Chair**, and the second **Axe** smashed the first

Hourglass whilst the second **Camel's Double Hump** carried the second **Hourglass**.

Example 9: Password Length = 12 characters
Password: 205833761216
Peg Words: 2-0-5-8-3-3-7-6-1-2-1-6

first Swan	Egg
Hook	Hourglass
first Camel's Double Hump	second Camel's Double Hump
Axe	first Golf Club
first Pen	second Swan
second Pen	second Golf Club

Sentence(s):
The first **Swan** was sitting on the **Egg** and the **Hook** was attached to the **Hourglass** whilst the **Axe** was swinging between the first **Camel's Double Hump** and second **Camel's Double Hump** on a rope, and the first **Golf Club** smashed the first **Pen,** and the second **Swan** was holding the second **Pen** in its beak whilst the second **Golf Club** was leaning against the wall.

Example 10: Password Length = 13 characters
Password: 7524835744538
Peg Words: 7-5-2-4-8-3-5-7-4-4-5-3-8

first Axe	first Hook
Swan	first Chair
first Hourglass	first Camel's Double Hump
second Hook	second Axe
second Chair	third Chair
third Hook	second Camel's Double Hump
second Hourglass	

Sentence(s):

The first **Axe** was hanging from the first **Hook** on the wall, and the **Swan** was sitting on the first **Chair** whilst the first **Hourglass** was resting on the first **Camel's Double Hump**, and the second **Hook** was also holding the second **Axe** on the wall, and the second **Chair** and the third **Chair** were attached by rope to the third **Hook** whilst the second **Camel's Double Hump** was holding the second **Hourglass**.

Example 11: Password Length = 14 characters
Password: 98495593792847
Peg Words: 9-8-4-9-5-5-9-3-7-9-2-8-4-7

first Tadpole	first Hourglass
first Chair	second Tadpole
first Hook	second Hook
third Tadpole	Camel's Double Hump
first Axe	fourth Tadpole
Swan	second Hourglass
second Chair	second Axe

Sentence(s):

The first **Tadpole** was resting on the first **Hourglass** on the first **Chair**, and the second **Tadpole** was hanging on a thread between the first **Hook** and second **Hook**, whilst the third **Tadpole** was on the **Camel's Double Hump**, and the first **Axe** cut the **Tadpole** into two, the **Swan** had one leg on the second **Hourglass** whilst the second **Chair** was lying on the second **Axe** on the floor.

Example 12: Password Length = 15 characters
Password: 184752976248207
Peg Words: 1-8-4-7-5-2-9-7-6-2-4-8-2-0-7

Pen	first Hourglass
first Chair	first Axe

Hook

Tadpole

Golf Club

second Chair

third Swan

third Axe

first Swan

second Axe

second Swan

second Hourglass

Egg

Sentence(s):

The **Pen** was lying near the first **Hourglass** on the table, the first **Chair** and first **Axe** were hanging on the **Hook**, and the first **Swan** swallowed the **Tadpole**, and the second **Axe** and **Golf Club** were lying on the floor, and the second **Swan** was standing on the second **Chair** and the second **Hourglass** was in the beak of the third **Swan**, which was sitting on the **Egg** near the third **Axe** on the ground.

Example 13: Password Length = 16 characters
Password: 8063034245458243
Peg Words: 8-0-6-3-0-3-4-2-4-5-4-5-8-2-4-3

first Hourglass

Golf Club

second Egg

first Chair

second Chair

third Chair

second Hourglass

fourth Chair

first Egg

first Camel's Double Hump

second Camel's Double Hump

first Swan

first Hook

second Hook

second Swan

third Camel's Double Hump

Sentence(s):

The first **Hourglass** was used to time when the first **Egg** was hatched, the **Golf Club** was hanging from the first **Camel's Double Hump**, and the second **Egg** was on the second **Camel's Double Hump** whilst on the first **Chair** was sitting the first **Swan**, and the second **Chair** was attached to the first **Hook** and the third

Chair to the second **Hook**, the second **Hourglass** was lying on the floor whilst the second **Swan** was standing on the fourth **Chair**, looking at the third **Camel's Double Hump**.

Example 14:   Password Length = 17 characters
Password: 07383534688424952
Peg Words: 0-7-3-8-3-5-3-4-6-8-8-4-2-4-9-5-2

Egg	Axe
first Camel's Double Hump	first Hourglass
second Camel's Double Hump	first Hook
third Camel's Double Hump	first Chair
Golf Club	second Hourglass
third Hourglass	second Chair
first Swan	third Chair
Tadpole	second Hook
second Swan	

Sentence(s):

The **Egg** was smashed with the **Axe**, the first **Camel's Double Hump** was carrying the first **Hourglass**, and the second **Camel's Double Hump** was attached to the first **Hook,** which was also attached to the third **Camel's Double Hump** whilst under the first **Chair** were lying the **Golf Club** and the second **Hourglass**, and the third **Hourglass** was on the second **Chair**, the first **Swan** was sitting on the third **Chair** whilst the **Tadpole** was hanging from the second **Hook**, and the second **Swan** was stretching its neck to pick it with its beak.

Example 15:   Password Length = 18 characters
Password: 622502388054201178
Peg Words: 6-2-2-5-0-2-3-8-8-0-5-4-2-0-1-1-7-8

Golf Club	first Swan
second Swan	first Hook

first Egg
Camel's Double Hump
second Hourglass
second Hook
fourth Swan
first Pen
Axe

third Swan
first Hourglass
second Egg
Chair
third Egg
second Pen
third Hourglass

Sentence(s):

The **Golf Club** was held in the beaks of the first **Swan** and the second **Swan**, the **Hook** was attached to the first **Egg** of the third **Swan** whilst the **Camel's Double Hump** was carrying the first **Hourglass** and the second **Hourglass**, and the second **Egg** was attached to the second **Hook** and the **Chair** on which the fourth **Swan** was standing with the third **Egg** in its beak whilst the first **Pen** and the second **Pen** were on the table, and the **Axe** and the third **Hourglass** were on the floor.

Example 16:   Password Length = 19 characters
Password: 9798105578681744051
Peg Words: 9-7-9-8-10-5-5-7-8-6-8-1-7-4-4-0-5-1

first Tadpole
second Tadpole
Fork And Plate
second Hook
second Hourglass
third Hourglass
third Axe
second Chair
third Hook

first Axe
first Hourglass
first Hook
second Axe
Golf Club
first Pen
first Chair
Egg
second Pen

Sentence(s):

The first **Tadpole** was lying on the first **Axe** and the second **Tadpole** was on the first **Hourglass**, the **Fork And Plate** were attached to the first **Hook**, and the second **Hook**, the second **Axe** and the second **Hourglass** were in the box, and the **Golf Club** broke the third **Hourglass**, the first **Pen** was cut into two with the third **Axe**, and the first **Chair** and the second **Chair** were near the table on which the **Egg** was lying, together with the third **Hook** and second **Pen**.

Example 17:   Password Length = 20 characters
Password: 09264601607425957859
Peg Words: 0-9-2-6-4-6-0-1-6-0-7-4-2-5-9-5-7-8-5-9

first Egg	first Tadpole
first Swan	first Golf Club
first Chair	second Golf Club
second Egg	Pen
third Golf Club	third Egg
first Axe	second Chair
second Swan	first Hook
second Tadpole	second Hook
second Axe	Hourglass
third Hook	second Tadpole

Sentence(s):

The first **Egg** rolled over the first **Tadpole**, the first **Swan** was hit with the first **Golf Club**, the first **Chair** was standing near the second **Golf Club**, the second **Egg** was pierced with the **Pen**, the third **Golf Club** smashed the third **Egg** and the first **Axe** was used to cut the second **Chair** into pieces.

The second **Swan** had the first **Hook** in its beak to which the second **Tadpole** was attached, the second **Hook** was holding the second **Axe** on the wall, the **Hourglass** was hanging from the third **Hook** and the second **Tadpole** was wriggling on the floor.

Example 18:   Password Length = 21 characters
Password: 787375441658190485989
Peg Words: 7-8-7-3-7-5-4-4-1-6-5-8-1-9-0-4-8-5-9-8-9

first Axe	first Hourglass
second Axe	Camel's Double Hump
third Axe	first Hook
first Chair	second Chair
first Pen	Golf Club
second Hook	second Hourglass
second Pen	first Tadpole
Egg	third Chair
third Hourglass	third Hook
second Tadpole	fourth Hourglass
third Tadpole	

Sentence(s):

The first **Axe** smashed the first **Hourglass**, the second **Axe** was lying on the **Camel's Double Hump**, the third **Axe** was attached to the first **Hook** and the first **Chair** and second **Chair**, the first **Pen** and the **Golf Club** were hanging from the second **Hook** and the second **Hourglass** and the second **Pen** were on the table.

The first **Tadpole** was sitting on the **Egg**, the third **Chair** and third **Hourglass** were attached to the third **Hook**, the second **Tadpole** was on the fourth **Hourglass** whilst the third **Tadpole** was on the floor.

Example 19:   Password Length = 22 characters
Password: 2141877454706836240899
Peg Words: 2-1-4-1-8-7-7-4-5-4-7-0-6-8-3-6-2-4-0-8-9-9

first Swan	first Pen
first Chair	second Pen
first Hourglass	first Axe
second Axe	second Chair

Hook	third Chair
third Axe	first Egg
first Golf Club	second Hourglass
Camel's Double Hump	second Golf Club
second Swan	fourth Chair
second Egg	third Hourglass
first Tadpole	second Tadpole

Sentence(s):

The first **Swan** was holding the first **Pen** in its beak, on the first **Chair** was the second **Pen**, the first **Hourglass** was smashed with the first **Axe**, the second **Axe** and the second **Chair** were both attached to the **Hook**, and the third **Chair** has fallen over and the third **Axe** has broken the first **Egg**.

The first **Golf Club** hit the second **Hourglass** and broke it, on the **Camel's Double Hump** was the second **Golf Club**, the second **Swan** was sitting on the fourth **Chair**, the second **Egg** was lying close to the third **Hourglass**, and the first **Tadpole** and second **Tadpole** were swimming in a glass of water.

Example 20: Password Length = 23 characters
Password: 74385224234592434238004
Peg Words: 7-4-3-8-5-2-2-4-2-3-4-5-9-2-4-3-4-2-3-8-0-0-4

Axe	first Chair
first Camel's Double Hump	first Hourglass
first Hook	first Swan
second Swan	second Chair
third swan	second Camel's Double Hump
third Chair	second Hook
Tadpole	fourth Swan
fourth Chair	third Camel's Double Hump
fifth Chair	fifth Swan
fourth Camel's Double Hump	second Hourglass

first Egg   second Egg
sixth Chair

Sentence(s):

The **Axe** smashed the first **Chair**, the first **Camel's Double Hump** carried the first **Hourglass**, the first **Hook** was attached to the beaks of the first **Swan** and second **Swan**, on the second **Chair** sat the third **Swan** and the second **Camel's Double Hump** and the third **Chair** were attached to the second **Hook**.

The **Tadpole** was swallowed by the fourth **Swan**, the fourth **Chair** was on the third **Camel's Double Hump**, on the fifth **Chair** stood the fifth **Swan**, the fourth **Camel's Double Hump** carried the second **Hourglass** and the first **Egg** and the second **Egg** were on the sixth **Chair**.

Example 21:   Password Length = 24 characters
Password: 420910739285953562709288
Peg Words: 4-2-0-9-10-7-3-9-2-8-5-9-5-3-5-6-2-7-0-9-2-8-8

Chair	first Swan
first Egg	first Tadpole
Fork And Plate	first Axe
first Camel's Double Hump	second Tadpole
second Swan	first Hourglass
first Hook	third Tadpole
second Hook	second Camel's Double Hump
third Hook	Golf Club
third Swan	second Axe
second Egg	fourth Tadpole
fourth Swan	second Hourglass
third Hourglass	

Sentence(s):

On the **Chair** sat the first **Swan** with the first **Egg** in its beak, the first **Tadpole** was lying near the **Fork And Plate**, which were then smashed with the first **Axe**, on the first **Camel's Double Hump** was the second **Tadpole**, the second **Swan** was holding the first **Hourglass** in its beak, and the first **Hook** was attached to the third **Tadpole**.

The second **Hook** was attached to the second **Camel's Double Hump**, the third **Hook** was attached to the **Golf Club**, the third **Swan** was standing over the second **Axe**, the second **Egg** rolled towards the fourth **Tadpole**, and the fourth **Swan** was standing between the second **Hourglass** and the third **Hourglass**.

Example 22:   Password Length = 25 characters
Password: 3227612247989106857075233
Peg Words: 3-2-2-7-6-1-2-2-4-7-9-8-9-10-6-8-5-7-0-7-5-2-3-3

first Camel's Double Hump	first Swan
second Swan	first Axe
first Golf Club	Pen
third Swan	fourth Swan
Chair	second Axe
first Tadpole	first Hourglass
second Tadpole	Fork And Plate
second Golf Club	second Hourglass
first Hook	third Axe
Egg	fourth Axe
second Hook	fifth Swan
second Camel's Double Hump	third Camel's Double Hump

Sentence(s):
On the first **Camel's Double Hump** sat the first **Swan** and the second **Swan**, the first **Axe** was lying close to the first **Golf Club**, the **Pen** was in the beak of the third **Swan**, the fourth **Swan** was standing on the **Chair**, the second **Axe** cut the first **Tadpole** into two and nearly damaged the first **Hourglass**.

The second **Tadpole** was wriggling towards the **Fork And Plate**, the second **Gulf Club** smashed the second **Hourglass**, the first **Hook** was attached to the third **Axe**, the **Egg** was destroyed by the fourth **Axe**, and the second **Hook** was attached to the fifth **Swan**, the second **Camel's Double Hump** and the third **Camel's Double Hump**.

2.2 Number Shape Practice Exercises

Exercises 1:   Password Length = 4 characters
5336
8917
7370
6706
8016
3788
9323
0203
7039
2737

Exercises 2:   Password Length = 5 characters
93649
93808
27373
94369
73798
87244
87359
24264
84847
75022

Exercises 3:   Password Length = 6 characters
223780

166332
679234
674132
396614
470655
007152
352541
176276
212612

Exercises 4:   Password Length = 7 characters
9531285
6707357
9188410
0004851
0212828
3699691
2932587
6145494
5224140
3310911

Exercises 5:   Password Length = 8 characters
26519931
31635398
27147153
85648397
61364429
61186640
12672648
25041219
56191094
34866682

Exercises 6:   Password Length = 9 characters
212840959

773347538
316420053
687358992
529380265
131307353
835292359
086286952
821950302
503530186

Exercises 7:   Password Length = 10 characters

8760756846
9727755067
7757177814
0713925313
2569568809
3080577971
6307098154
6410710323
6428309478
0788536488

Exercises 8:   Password Length = 11 characters

18209949750
45570828373
69888978504
09163411322
64898654200
95684976836
58718792317
74851947660
34273428916
20266297805

Exercises 9:   Password Length = 12 characters

234367125975

757307994945
988787620654
774270346128
592551320289
934420269836
452168515909
756949489992
306685101359
332371447978

Exercises 10:   Password Length = 13 characters
3228710598548
3904783688865
1043551282881
2199891057798
7533273501102
6270824393228
9398442238878
2936967748218
0453986959602
2483964562423

Exercises 11:   Password Length = 14 characters
90106993420692
33912145749067
87713262600198
19563448147178
35078694163713
95454631928772
96501809321025
25123358485026
05535787162091
08039876554696

Exercises 12:   Password Length = 15 characters
873633068935446

859179483623480
477741447456243
496535530145095
814228559886104
617173168052097
451275780711799
514055700503841
241738556096373
638879052857011

Exercises 13: Password Length = 16 characters

1334122899768326
8321346664863914
9561708882816856
3117414975505571
5756650997115669
5749703568406022
8774648113061957
8946239843715540
4682713295760499
7454723273288843

Exercises 14: Password Length = 17 characters

24474866590317317
23627999901415205
63661431028958192
08921165377892500
75361654595541677
89913550941205871
02687939839284603
21124069759321499
76389333281926389
13563096721950556

Exercises 15: Password Length = 18 characters

088817211386829244

668767780006112229
151758288767079306
613326257531160757
233277598392338164
930330052173979694
643840662635459178
713208104319855330
692323284125329401
240111377627456656

Exercises 16:   Password Length = 19 characters
2861206646041429337
6776353832239959610
2441698277740067700
3741934563522484685
9670292296669785070
7059910462873916816
0839048539826882776
2114247802230119222
5735766015592322211
8344685376076911101

Exercises 17:   Password Length = 20 characters
86103101268524287870
28275872880992205564
08590250637663176251
85524164064451495518
08673894119039998943
90072835569868388377
36994770488407450988
87630304934273771635
46153433585364787144
04363350659399874839

Exercises 18:   Password Length = 21 characters
915356445234831670894

596402941142191129250
092634816017071046141
102356709316024757223
943155307096977343522
207222565487128208399
856862029590929371752
897203317528912041153
782621486507947385319
308673337380776357019

Exercises 19:   Password Length = 22 characters
2825206888535507141037
9165940804848803877212
2903547927710444026764
7670366804436561788176
4258996152781751710803
9374782330950145301635
2371899618542771009971
6570488599712480985965
3818216218108835512892
6641658275266191413517

Exercises 20:   Password Length = 23 characters
97337012929599159102469
91224821883469882992479
89823704900488735975559
31712881302086108712923
47760356789354581244991
56432337830685859285819
46762275661408026120723
44592875265524372364916
48044871674280925224627
60506478746412218802859

Exercises 21:   Password Length = 24 characters
908887221236191711421126

46

23457221397522168097618
22352881716592149866991
34537031225041647719965
21678181498617460244632
18897951097246028274294
83500784355605700814982
60381286627730258714004
34875629225334066848292
10344039438657466751915

Exercises 22:   Password Length = 25 characters
2501624444359636134352813
63819048861641956983800589
2659998532429689686648252
3691596262479631963394102
0099485547423158892106077
5886750324326564097598475
1573216223309307582662886
7729482766655168239468594
0663231228045226753067053
5979685548163144639095066

Chapter 3

Phonetic Number System

In this system, each number is associated with one or more consonants. The vowels, a, e, i, o, u, and the alphabets, w, h, y, and x, are not linked to any number. These unassigned alphabets could be used to form words. However, the phonetic complexities associated with knowing the difference between a soft c sound and a hard c sound, a soft ch sound and hard ch sound, a soft g sound and hard g sound from the lists of consonants have been removed from this classification to simplify things. Some people create lists based on these peculiarities which I think is unnecessarily complex, daunting and discouraging for the diffident and uninitiated in English phonetics. I think we should not worry ourselves with linguistic complexities which lie within the purview of linguistic experts.

This is why I have decided to use this simplified list of consonants below:

Numbers and Associated Consonants

Table 3.1: Numbers and Associated Consonants

Number	Associated Consonant(s)
0	s, z
1	t, d
2	n
3	m
4	r
5	l
6	j, ch, sh

7	k, g, c, q
8	f, v
9	p, b

If you memorize the numbers and the associated consonants, you can encode any number using the given peg words. You can also use this list of numbers and associated consonants to form any number of peg words you like. We are going to use these to produce one hundred peg words that we can use to memorize long lists. If we want to find a peg word for the number, 0, we know that the number 0 is represented by the letter s and z, and we can use any of the vowels, a, e, i, o, u, and the letters w, h, y, and x to form words. So an example of a peg word for 0 is SEA. We will follow this principle and form peg words for the other numbers as follows:

Table 3.2: Phonetic Number Peg Words

Number	Peg Word	Number	Peg Word
0	Sea	50	Lazy
1	Tow	51	Lathe
2	New	52	Lane
3	Mow	53	Lame
4	Row	54	Lair
5	Law	55	Lily
6	Shoe	56	Leash
7	Key	57	Log
8	Eve	58	Loaf
9	Bow	59	Loop
10	Dose	60	Jews
11	Dude	61	Cheat
12	Tone	62	Chain

13	Tome	63	Shame
14	Door	64	Jar
15	Tool	65	Shoal
16	Touch	66	Joshua
17	Toke	67	Jug
18	Dove	68	Chafe
19	Dope	69	Chip
20	Nose	70	Goose
21	Newt	71	Cat
22	Nun	72	Goon
23	Nome	73	Game
24	Nero	74	Queer
25	Nail	75	Keel
26	Nosh	76	Cushaw
27	Nuke	77	Cog
28	Nave	78	Cave
29	Nape	79	Cab
30	Moose	80	Vows
31	Meat	81	Foot
32	Mane	82	Vane
33	Mom	83	Fame
34	Moor	84	Fur
35	Mole	85	Fool
36	Mush	86	Vouchee
37	Mug	87	Fog
38	Move	88	Five
39	Mob	89	Fop
40	Rose	90	Pose
41	Road	91	Pod
42	Rain	92	Phone
43	Ram	93	Beam

44	Rare	94	Poor
45	Rail	95	Pool
46	Rash	96	Bush
47	Rage	97	Book
48	Rave	98	Poof
49	Rape	99	Pub

Some people have used this method to create hundreds and thousands of peg words which they memorize and use in diverse ways. However, I do not think we need to do that unless we are training to become memory contest champions.

As you can see, you can code a lot of passwords using these peg words to form sentences which you can then memorize and use to recall the original passwords.

Learning Procedure

1. You memorize the numbers and their associated peg words. Memorize them very well through repetition and reinforcement because you will always have to remember them in order to recall the passwords.
2. You find the peg words for the numbers in the password and arrange them in the order in which they appear in the password.
3. You construct sentences with the peg words in order to chain or link them sequentially and coherently together. The more outrageous a sentence is, the easier it is for you to remember it.
4. You memorize the sentences in order to get the correct positions of the peg words in the sentences with absolute ease.
5. You will then be able to remember the password if you remember the numbers and their associated peg words.

How to Memorize the Sentences Constructed with the Peg Words

You will use repetition and reinforcement to learn these sentences.

1.   Read the sentences inaudibly five or ten times.
2.   Read the sentences audibly five or ten times.
3.   Write down the sentences five or ten times.

Please continue this process till you can easily remember the sentences.

Please note that we have used the uppercase for initial letters of specific words or specific words in the groups of words in the sentences constructed in this book and bolded them only for emphasis and clarity. We crave your indulgence if you are unhappy that this may be an irremissible infraction of the rules of grammar.

3.1 Phonetic Number Examples

Example 1:   Password Length = 4 characters
Password: 8045
Peg Words: 80-45
 Vows   Rail
Sentence(s):
The couple made their **Vows** on the **Rail** road in the presence of family members and well-wishers.

Example 2:   Password Length = 5 characters
Password: 13573
Peg Words: 1-35-73
 Tow   Mole   Game

Sentence(s):

The tugboat gave the yacht a **Tow** to the **Mole** on the beach where the **Game** warden was standing and watching them.

Example 3: Password Length = 6 characters
Password: 548022
Peg Words: 54-80-22

Lair   Vows   Nun

Sentence(s):

The **Lair** of the foxes was close to where the **Vows** were said by the **Nun**.

Example 4: Password Length = 7 characters
Password: 0795852
Peg Words: 0-79-58-52

Sea   Cab   Loaf
Lane

Sentence(s):

At the **Sea** front, the driver parked his **Cab** in order to **Loaf** around in the **Lane** which branched off the coastal drive.

Example 5: Password Length = 8 characters
Password: 76016735
Peg Words: 76-0-1-67-35

Cushaw   Sea   Tow
Jug   Mole

Sentence(s):

The **Cushaw** plant was growing close to the **Sea** where the driver of the **Tow** truck had stopped to drink a **Jug** of hot tea in the presence of the Russian **Mole** he was to contact.

Example 6:   Password Length = 9 characters
Password: 463571401
Peg Words: 46-35-71-40-1

Rash	Mole	Cat
Rose	Tow	

Sentence(s):

A sudden **Rash** appeared on the arm of the **Mole** when the **Cat** rubbed itself against him at the window overlooking the **Rose** tree where the **Tow** truck had been parked.

Example 7:   Password Length = 10
Password: 7532962346
Peg Words: 75-32-96-23-46

Keel	Mane	Bush
Nome	Rash	

Sentence(s):

The **Keel** on the breastbone of the small bird rubbed the **Mane** of the horse when it flew low to pick a mite from the back of the horse in a **Bush** in **Nome**, in western Alaska, where the community had developed a **Rash**.

Example 8:   Password Length = 11 characters
Password: 81299773629
Peg Words: 8-12-99-77-36-29

Eve	Tone	Pub
Cog	Mush	Nape

Sentence(s):

Eve sang a song with a beautiful **Tone** in the **Pub** where she was a small **Cog** in the administrative setup, and afterwards she went to the kitchen to eat **Mush** pulling the collar of her coat to cover her **Nape**.

Example 9:   Password Length = 12 characters
Password: 680932218930
Peg Words: 6-80-9-32-21-89-30

Shoe	Vows	Bow
Mane	Newt	Fop
Moose		

Sentence(s):

With the **Shoe** in her hand, after making her **Vows** in church, she greeted the man with the **Bow** and arrow in his hand, sitting on the horse with the golden **Mane** whilst the **Newt** was crawling away from the **Fop** on the other side of the road quite close to the **Moose** hiding in the bush.

Example 10:   Password Length = 13 characters
Password: 9220680177796
Peg Words: 92-20-6-80-17-77-96

Phone	Nose	Shoe
Vows	Toke	Cog
Bush		

Sentence(s):

He rubbed his **Phone** against the side of his **Nose**, holding in his hand the **Shoe** he had made **Vows** not to touch, then taking a **Toke** on a joint he was smoking, where a **Cog** on the gear wheel lying down in the **Bush** had scratched him on an earlier visit there.

Example 11:   Password Length = 14 characters
Password: 35413800851725
Peg Words: 3-54-13-80-0-85-17-25

Mow	Lair	Tome
Vows	Sea	Fool
Toke	Nail	

Sentence(s):

The **Mow** in the barn was the **Lair** of the author who wrote a **Tome** on taking matrimonial **Vows** at **Sea** and always detested the **Fool** who just took a **Toke** on a joint and has a long **Nail** on his little finger.

Example 12:   Password Length = 15 characters
Password: 872406738342350
Peg Words: 8-72-40-67-38-34-23-50

Eve	Goon	Rose
Jug	Move	Moor
Nome	Lazy	

Sentence(s):

Eve loved the **Goon** who always had a **Rose** in his breast pocket and was always drinking a **Jug** of milk, and was delighted by the **Move** of the **Moor** to go to **Nome**, in western Alaska, where no one would chastise him for being **Lazy**.

Example 13:   Password Length = 16 characters
Password: 2862045763966489
Peg Words: 28-62-0-4-57-63-96-64-89

Nave	Chain	Sea
Row	Log	Shame
Bush	Jar	Fop

Sentence(s):

The **Nave** of the church, which had a **Chain** in front and was close to the **Sea,** was where there was the **Row** on the **Log** of the ship, which brought **Shame** to the community, because it was the catalogue of the happenings in the **Bush** on the island the sailors had explored and the **Jar** of honey demanded by the **Fop**.

Example 14: Password Length = 17 characters
Password: 90345929817697409
Peg Words: 90-34-59-29-81-76-97-40-9

Pose	Moor	Loop
Nape	Foot	Cushaw
Book	Rose	Bow

Sentence(s):

The **Pose** of the **Moor** showed his arrogance of being in the **Loop** of the president's confidantes, and pulling the collar of his suit over his **Nape** with a **Foot** on a stool reading about the **Cushaw** plant in a black **Book**, he rearranged the **Rose** in his breast pocket and straightened his **Bow** tie.

Example 15: Password Length = 18 characters
Password: 760487043173659437
Peg Words: 7-60-48-70-4-31-73-65-94-37

Key	Jews	Rave
Goose	Row	Meat
Game	Shoal	Poor
Mug		

Sentence(s):

He had the **Key** to the house of the **Jews** in his pocket whilst dancing at the **Rave,** where roasted **Goose** and a **Row** of all types of **Meat** presented by the **Game** warden were served, and a **Shoal** of gold fish were swimming in the indoor aquarium in the hall whilst the **Poor** caretaker stood nearby nursing a **Mug** of coffee.

Example 16: Password Length = 19 characters
Password: 6526738596288376489
Peg Words: 6-52-67-38-59-62-88-37-64-89

Shoe	Lane	Jug

Move	Loop	Chain
Five	Mug	Jar
Fop		

Sentence(s):

He laced his **Shoe**, went onto the **Lane**, holding a **Jug** of orange juice, made a **Move** around the **Loop**, holding the **Chain** for support and came to the **Five** men, each holding a **Mug** and a **Jar** of honey, given to them by the **Fop**.

Example 17:   Password Length = 20 characters
Password: 49584333028209989403
Peg Words: 4-95-84-33-30-28-20-99-89-40-3

Row	Pool	Fur
Mom	Moose	Nave
Nose	Pub	Fop
Rose	Mow	

Sentence(s):

A **Row** ensued near the **Pool** where the **Fur** coat of a **Mom** made from **Moose**, which she had pulled up her **Nape**, smelled so badly that it offended the **Nose** of each of the guests in the **Pub** owned by the **Fop**, who always had a **Rose** in his breast pocket and regularly takes a nap in the **Mow** in the barn.

Example 18:   Password Length = 21 characters
Password: 491174729264177801939
Peg Words: 4-91-17-47-29-26-41-77-80-19-39

Row	Pod	Toke
Rage	Nape	Nosh
Road	Cog	Vows
Dope	Mob	

Sentence(s):

There was a **Row** over the **Pod**, which got detached from the airplane and fell down, where the mechanic had taken a single **Toke** on the joint smoked by the cleaner, who went into a **Rage** because someone had hit him on the **Nape**, when he was eating his **Nosh** on the side of the street.

The **Road** led to the place where the **Cog** on the gear wheel had scratched his leg, and he had made his **Vows** to become a faithful supplier of **Dope** for the **Mob**.

Example 19: Password Length = 22 characters
Password: 2966705501601527205190
Peg Words: 29-66-70-5-50-1-60-15-27-20-51-90

Nape	Joshua	Goose
Law	Lazy	Tow
Jews	Tool	Nuke
Nose	Lathe	Pose

Sentence(s):

The **Nape** of **Joshua** was scratched by the flying **Goose** whilst the **Law** was being read to the **Lazy** driver of the **Tow** truck, which was owned by the **Jews** in the neighborhood.

The **Tool** he was taking to the **Nuke** to repair its damaged **Nose** was manufactured on this **Lathe** machine operated by the technician who was standing in an unnatural **Pose** in one corner of the workshop.

Example 20: Password Length = 23 characters
Password: 59536587730173271336483
Peg Words: 5-95-36-58-77-30-17-32-71-33-64-83

Law	Pool	Mush
Loaf	Cog	Moose
Toke	Mane	Cat

Mom	Jar	Fame

Sentence(s):

The chairman enacted his own **Law** to control the **Pool** of companies under his command, went out and gave some **Mush** and a **Loaf** of bread to the man who was an essential **Cog** in the administrative setup of the consortium.

The man shot the **Moose** with his rifle, took a **Toke** on his joint, rubbed contentedly his **Mane** of auburn hair, went home and stroked the **Cat** of his **Mom**, who was eating from a **Jar** and reading about the **Fame** of one of the top celebrities in the country.

Example 21: Password Length = 24 characters
Password: 842982162219267774531191
Peg Words: 84-29-82-16-22-19-26-77-74-53-11-91

Fur	Nape	Vane
Touch	Nun	Dope
Nosh	Cog	Queer
Lame	Dude	Pod

Sentence(s):

He had pulled the **Fur** coat over his **Nape** and lifted his eyes to look at the **Vane** in order to check the direction of the wind, when he felt the **Touch** of the **Nun** on his arm to inform him about the **Dope** which the police had confiscated.

The **Nosh** the small **Cog** in the administrative setup of the organization brought to him to pacify him was considered a **Queer** and **Lame** excuse by the **Dude** to appease him before repairing the damaged **Pod** of the airplane.

Example 22: Password Length = 25 characters
Password: 4617483626360945562917700
Peg Words: 4-61-74-83-62-63-60-9-45-56-29-17-70-0

Row	Cheat	Queer
Fame	Chain	Shame
Jews	Bow	Rail
Leash	Nape	Toke
Goose	Sea	

Sentence(s):

The **Row** between the **Cheat** and the **Queer** over the **Fame** of the entrepreneur who owned the **Chain** of stores was considered a **Shame** by the **Jews**.

The actors took a **Bow** before the **Rail** on stage when acknowledging the applause of the audience, one of them holding a **Leash** attached to the dog which featured in the drama, another pulled his coat over his **Nape** and took a **Toke** on a fake joint with a large image of the **Goose** and the **Sea** in the background.

3.2 Phonetic Number Practice Exercises

Exercises 1:   Password Length = 4 characters

8732
9977
2686
5871
4919
9001
6323
9269
7268
8761

Exercises 2:   Password Length = 5 characters

14068
51780
36694

44585
10278
93688
06747
37487
48608
16780

Exercises 3:   Password Length = 6 characters
717093
474463
679779
579409
582156
709051
763981
464855
076736
788640

Exercises 4:   Password Length = 7 characters
4139836
2062502
0654781
7873799
9986163
4761610
9299219
5470945
5690572
7615052

Exercises 5:   Password Length = 8 characters
14739327
20616201
49758183

73269790
74920785
12413853
11684100
14701507
53253784
11349837

Exercises 6: Password Length = 9 characters
018835058
514606506
449534417
546329387
317274874
843957255
048006619
228326169
739582064
725360139

Exercises 7: Password Length = 10 characters
0816690217
8121715125
4551649537
7044182387
6715523950
0867618133
8614983992
8879201019
8243878564
3202158972

Exercises 8: Password Length = 11 characters
40720563511
56980486588
33322376139

51427503645
15576961052
38781773928
14640339036
45380156945
54670281883
39133550461

Exercises 9:   Password Length = 12 characters
219269405863
928039191829
108030328766
065668155572
489634318434
936758720821
208274995620
200273359368
723840493672
701467164356

Exercises 10:   Password Length = 13 characters
0817227446012
0745700990756
5708776114906
9835785503765
0738790800539
4578881907637
7888982233657
4084593103433
9510452931492
1626116154753

Exercises 11:   Password Length = 14 characters
34420914208595
30550030047105
09690097495847

11991539671144
28435806450307
68263894673543
73002510584168
22402533755835
43258052456480
05862886848730

Exercises 12: Password Length = 15 characters
872935707880502
241771037049990
591598621013629
572281687131131
506723888339801
757243099706613
113433688872683
216723478905332
056023659008702
344283084491711

Exercises 13: Password Length = 16 characters
4753765892472622
5890613621577591
0206373290498208
6166582322961289
5159589757480009
8945727651459530
6148361806756873
4777011116160172
4011893164471185
1442354191867378

Exercises 14: Password Length = 17 characters
16523191390129504
01012909250605688
44697072354967207

02800350102554245
59094030590925579
65606982092511959
37159635794059405
59599605523477501
57135850016681869
46614816358603821

Exercises 15:   Password Length = 18 characters

230935565003839591
960425560099497586
551745349230183531
770294346790700864
672432380384808883
726022873620243333
207297999078826858
667242598900092275
937585670687131992
271754122033481391

Exercises 16:   Password Length = 19 characters

1161448731140550764
9070485424838603532
0413976500812525746
7258840975590815080
2423576129812556861
4688098597196161607
1832425412204537067
5156874309743670702
9419371519724504480
9234205094154816936

Exercises 17:   Password Length = 20 characters

04102328766814411712
25730559703795830467
80722818113704063536

89330834695904105867
34371728592875005943
53290874668087176476
72134077442317932651
44668314829476775964
96082772295585594259
25410714376478010551

Exercises 18: Password Length = 21 characters
573307312511312426573
104303938738934717917
442805570565575253794
394797422198231959599
700783134314790802623
215317130564908519888
985226674167139721127
244587390248875159697
987941538471435010459
691326825558769007332

Exercises 19: Password Length = 22 characters
8215539716884832992206
9150124597601596905235
5889936290691441123691
6692397810870071804070
0489551321601414810772
7328309997119237066814
8937235982098529208206
5752165460423538386579
8092608348082176128174
3190745392365987182207

Exercises 20: Password Length = 23 characters
84863228926712808527326
13867942434772890000890
53522047281437932249740

0196743129786062609325
7901361922666097977320
7250248298369138354365
5131796357359456952522
6323199621900332590346
2916822776521801933618
3392421064893191742755

Exercises 21: Password Length = 24 characters
391809211950783193547761
115525285905304374128246
558644749547469359852449
506064798758363490694854
339667591241060790723082
797877698366690336662794
149871023742200875458068
881587940609537287357575
142001299895389132078521
340111731366752257212418

Exercises 22: Password Length = 25 characters
1866170746281943127566270
6988120585957979112652838
6015019086204659880528235
2112755607653405158442712
8293752305002020069297307
2252827469922911996309192
5839131501391179332131931
0880070072248966162142462
3203036208838346177276136
7607479842620138719942824

Chapter 4

Number-Object Peg System

Objects, which have a numerical relationship with specific numbers in terms of the number of specific physical attributes they have, are linked together.

Examples are given below:

Table 4.1: Number-Object Peg Words

Number	Peg Word	Reason
0	Vacuum	No matter present, i.e., zero matter
1	Universe	There is only one (1) universe.
2	Pair of Dice	Two (2) dice
3	Pitchfork	Three (3) prongs
4	Dog	Four (4) legs
5	Hand	Five (5) fingers
6	Ant	Six (6) legs
7	Rainbow	Seven (7) colors
8	Stop Sign	Eight (8) sides
9	Baseball	Nine (9) players on a team with nine (9) innings
10	Dime	Ten (10) cents

Learning Procedure

1. You memorize the numbers and their associated peg words. Memorize them very well through repetition and

reinforcement because you will always have to remember them in order to recall the passwords.

2. You find the peg words for the numbers in the password and arrange them in the order in which they appear in the password.

3. You construct sentences with the peg words in order to chain or link them sequentially and coherently together. The more outrageous a sentence is, the easier it is for you to remember it.

4. You memorize the sentences in order to get the correct positions of the peg words in the sentences with absolute ease.

5. You will then be able to remember the password if you remember the numbers and their associated peg words.

How to Memorize the Sentences Constructed with the Peg Words

You will use repetition and reinforcement to learn these sentences.

1. Read the sentences inaudibly five or ten times.
2. Read the sentences audibly five or ten times.
3. Write down the sentences five or ten times.

Please continue this process till you can easily remember the sentences.

Please note that we have used the uppercase for initial letters of specific words or specific words in the groups of words in the sentences constructed in this book and bolded them only for emphasis and clarity. We crave your indulgence if you are unhappy that this may be an irremissible infraction of the rules of grammar.

4.1 Number-Object Examples

Example 1:   Password Length = 4 characters
Password: 2730
Peg Words: 2-7-3-0

Pair Of Dice	Rainbow
Pitchfork	Vacuum

Sentence(s):
The **Pair Of Dice** was thrown when the **Rainbow** appeared, and the **Pitchfork** was placed in front of the **Vacuum** chamber.

Example 2:   Password Length = 5 characters
Password: 90710
Peg Words: 9-0-7-10

Baseball	Vacuum
Rainbow	Dime

Sentence(s):
When the **Baseball** was thrown against the door of the **Vacuum** chamber, the **Rainbow** appeared in the sky and the **Dime** rolled away on the floor.

Example 3:   Password Length = 6 characters
Password: 983716
Peg Words: 9-8-3-7-1-6

Baseball	Stop Sign
Pitchfork	Rainbow
Universe	Ant

Sentence(s):
When the **Baseball** hit the **Stop Sign**, he raised the **Pitchfork** and pointed it at the **Rainbow**, and the **Universe** shone with a myriad of stars as the **Ant** ambled along the path.

Example 4:   Password Length = 7 characters
Password: 3074013
Peg Words: 3-0-7-4-0-1-3

first Pitchfork	first Vacuum
Rainbow	Dog
second Vacuum	Universe
second Pitchfork	

Sentence(s):

The first **Pitchfork** was thrown against the door of the first **Vacuum** chamber, the **Rainbow** appeared when the **Dog** was playing in front of the second **Vacuum** chamber, and the **Universe** displayed a constellation of stars shaped like the second **Pitchfork**.

Example 5:   Password Length = 8 characters
Password: 85755814
Peg Words: 8-5-7-5-5-8-1-4

first Stop Sign	first Hand
Rainbow	second Hand
third Hand	second Stop Sign
Universe	Dog

Sentence(s):

The first **Stop Sign** was close to the first **Hand** painted on the wall, and when the **Rainbow** appeared, he arrived at the place where the second **Hand** and the third **Hand** were being painted on the billboard near the second **Stop Sign**, and the **Universe** fascinated the **Dog** as it sat on its hunches and looked at it.

Example 6:   Password Length = 9 characters
Password: 074751049
Peg Words: 0-7-4-7-5-10-4-9

Vacuum	first Rainbow

first Dog	second Rainbow
Hand	Dime
second Dog	Baseball

Sentence(s):

Standing in front of the **Vacuum** chamber, he looked at the first **Rainbow**, the first **Dog** admired the second **Rainbow**, and his **Hand** was holding the **Dime** whilst the second **Dog** was carrying the **Baseball** bat in its mouth.

Example 7: Password Length = 10 characters
Password: 6895233524
Peg Words: 6-8-9-5-2-3-3-5-2-4

Ant	Stop Sign
Baseball	first Hand
first Pair Of Dice	first Pitchfork
second Pitchfork	second Hand
second Pair of Dice	Dog

Sentence(s):

The **Ant** was walking across the **Stop Sign**, the **Baseball** was thrown by the first **Hand**, the first **Pair Of Dice** was cast where the first **Pitchfork** and the second **Pitchfork** were lying, and the second **Hand** threw the second **Pair Of Dice** in front of the **Dog**, which was taking a nap on the floor.

Example 8: Password Length = 11 characters
Password: 37992266971
Peg Words: 3-7-9-9-2-2-6-6-9-7-1

Pitchfork	first Rainbow
first Baseball	second Baseball
first Pair of Dice	second Pair Of Dice
first Ant	second Ant
third Baseball	second Rainbow

Universe

Sentence(s):

He pointed the **Pitchfork** at the first **Rainbow**, and the first **Baseball** and the second **Baseball** were thrown as soon as the first **Pair Of Dice** and the second **Pair Of Dice** were cast, and the first **Ant** and the second **Ant** were walking towards the third **Baseball** as the second **Rainbow** appeared in the **Universe**.

Example 9:   Password Length = 12 characters
Password: 892677379392
Peg Words: 8-9-2-6-7-7-3-7-9-3-9-2

Stop Sign	first Baseball
first Pair Of Dice	Ant
first Rainbow	second Rainbow
first Pitchfork	third Rainbow
second Baseball	second Pitchfork
third Baseball	second Pair Of Dice

Sentence(s):

The **Stop Sign** was hit by the first **Baseball**, the first **Pair Of Dice** was thrown over the **Ant** as the first **Rainbow** and the second **Rainbow** appeared in the sky, and he stuck the first **Pitchfork** into the ground when the third **Rainbow** appeared, the second **Baseball** was thrown when the second **Pitchfork** was hurled into the bushes, and the third **Baseball** was thrown when the second **Pair Of Dice** was cast.

Example 10:   Password Length = 13 characters
Password: 6784783196509
Peg Words: 6-7-8-4-7-8-3-1-9-6-5-0-9

first Ant	first Rainbow
first Stop Sign	Dog
second Rainbow	second Stop Sign

Pitchfork	Universe
first Baseball	second Ant
Hand	Vacuum
second Baseball	

Sentence(s):

The first **Ant** looked at the first **Rainbow**, when the man reached the first **Stop Sign**, where the **Dog** was standing, the second **Rainbow** appeared when he arrived at the second **Stop Sign**, where the **Pitchfork** has been driven into the ground, and he looked at the **Universe** and threw the first **Baseball** at the second **Ant**, and there was a **Hand** painted on the door of the **Vacuum** chamber, from which the second **Baseball** was rolling towards him.

Example 11:   Password Length = 14 characters
Password: 52391103826597
Peg Words: 5-2-3-9-1-10-3-8-2-6-5-9-7

first Hand	first Pair Of Dice
first Pitchfork	first Baseball
Universe	Dime
second Pitchfork	Stop Sign
second Pair of Dice	Ant
second Hand	second Baseball
Rainbow	

Sentence(s):

The first **Hand** threw the first **Pair Of Dice**, the first **Pitchfork** was used to pierce the first **Baseball** under the **Universe**, the **Dime** was used to buy the second **Pitchfork**, and when he saw the **Stop Sign**, he threw the second **Pair Of Dice**, the **Ant** was walking towards the second **Hand** painted on the wall, and the second **Baseball** was thrown towards the **Rainbow** in the sky.

Example 12:   Password Length = 15 characters
Password: 227731882333732
Peg Words: 2-2-7-7-3-1-8-8-2-3-3-3-7-3-2

first Pair Of Dice	second Pair Of Dice
first Rainbow	second Rainbow
first Pitchfork	Universe
first Stop Sign	second Stop Sign
third Pair Of Dice	second Pitchfork
third Pitchfork	fourth Pitchfork
third Rainbow	fifth Pitchfork
fourth Pair Of Dice	

Sentence(s):

The first **Pair Of Dice** and the second **Pair Of Dice** were cast when the first **Rainbow** and the second **Rainbow** appeared in the sky, he picked the first **Pitchfork** looked at the **Universe** above and then walked to the first **Stop Sign** and the second **Stop Sign** and threw the third **Pair Of Dice**, and he later took the second **Pitchfork**, the third **Pitchfork** and the fourth **Pitchfork**, looked at the third **Rainbow**, then picked the fifth **Pitchfork** and cast the fourth **Pair Of Dice**.

Example 13:   Password Length = 16 characters
Password: 0866816751228581
Peg Words: 0-8-6-6-8-1-6-7-5-1-2-2-8-5-8-1

Vacuum	first Stop Sign
first Ant	second Ant
second Stop Sign	first Universe
third Ant	Rainbow
first Hand	second Universe
first Pair Of Dice	second Pair Of Dice
third Stop Sign	second Hand
fourth Stop Sign	third Universe

Sentence(s):

He left the first **Vacuum** chamber and came to the first **Stop Sign** where he saw the first **Ant** and the second **Ant**, he continued and came to the second **Stop Sign** and looked at the first **Universe**, he then saw the third **Ant**, the **Rainbow**, and the imprint of the first **Hand** on the second **Universe**, he threw the first **Pair Of Dice** and the second **Pair Of Dice** at the third **Stop Sign**, he saw the second **Hand** painted on the wall at the fourth **Stop Sign** and then looked at the third **Universe**.

Example 14:   Password Length = 17 characters
Password: 40443595607572861
Peg Words: 4-0-4-4-3-5-9-5-6-0-7-5-7-2-8-6-1

first Dog	first Vacuum
second Dog	third Dog
Pitchfork	first Hand
Baseball	second Hand
first Ant	second Vacuum
first Rainbow	third Hand
second Rainbow	Pair Of Dice
Stop Sign	second Ant
Universe	

Sentence(s):

The first **Dog** ran to the first **Vacuum** chamber, the second **Dog** and the third **Dog** ran to where the **Pitchfork** was lying on the ground, and the first **Hand** took the **Baseball** and threw it and the second **Hand** caught it after stepping over the first **Ant**, he left the second **Vacuum** chamber and saw the first **Rainbow**, the third **Hand**, the second **Rainbow** and the **Pair Of Dice**, and at the **Stop Sign**, he saw the second **Ant** watching the **Universe**.

Example 15:   Password Length = 18 characters
Password: 875791131899821334
Peg Words: 8-7-5-7-9-1-1-3-1-8-9-9-8-2-1-3-3-4

first Stop Sign	first Rainbow
Hand	second Rainbow
first Baseball	first Universe
second Universe	first Pitchfork
third Universe	second Stop Sign
second Baseball	third Baseball
third Stop Sign	Pair Of Dice
fourth Universe	second Pitchfork
third Pitchfork	Dog

Sentence(s):

He saw the first **Stop Sign**, the first **Rainbow** and the **Hand** painted on the wall before the second **Rainbow** appeared in the sky, and the first **Baseball** was hurled towards the first **Universe** and the second **Universe** before the first **Pitchfork** was thrown at the third **Universe**, he stopped at the second **Stop Sign** and threw the second **Baseball** and the third **Baseball** when he reached the third **Stop Sign**, and he then cast the **Pair Of Dice**, and looked at the fourth **Universe,** and hurled both the second **Pitchfork** and the third **Pitchfork** at the **Dog** which had bitten him.

Example 16:   Password Length = 19 characters
Password: 2691095250769635916
Peg Words: 2-6-9-10-9-5-2-5-0-7-6-9-6-3-5-9-1-6

first Pair Of Dice	first Ant
first Baseball	Dime
second Baseball	first Hand
second Pair Of Dice	second Hand
Vacuum	Rainbow
second Ant	third Baseball

third Ant	Pitchfork
third Hand	fourth Baseball
Universe	fourth Ant

Sentence(s):

The first **Pair Of Dice** was cast as the first **Ant** walked past, the first **Baseball** bounced over the **Dime**, the second **Baseball** was thrown by the first **Hand**, and the second **Pair Of Dice** was cast by the second **Hand** before the door of the **Vacuum** chamber as the **Rainbow** appeared in the sky, and the second **Ant** was on top of the third **Baseball**, the third **Ant** was walking on the **Pitchfork**, the third **Hand** threw the fourth **Baseball**, and the **Universe** became dark as the fourth **Ant** stood still and watched.

Example 17:   Password Length = 20
Password: 96156022435560372589
Peg Words: 9-6-1-5-6-0-2-2-4-3-5-5-6-0-3-7-2-5-8-9

first Baseball	first Ant
Universe	first Hand
second Ant	first Vacuum
first Pair Of Dice	second Pair Of Dice
Dog	first Pitchfork
second Hand	third Hand
third Ant	second Vacuum
second Pitchfork	Rainbow
third Pair Of Dice	fourth Hand
Stop Sign	second Baseball

Sentence(s):

The first **Baseball** rolled over the first **Ant** as it looked at the **Universe**, the first **Hand** hit the second **Ant** on the door of the first **Vacuum** chamber, he threw the first **Pair Of Dice** and the second **Pair Of Dice** as the **Dog** barked, and the first **Pitchfork** was in the second **Hand**.

The third **Hand** covered the third **Ant** on the door of the second **Vacuum** chamber, he put the second **Pitchfork** down as the **Rainbow** appeared in the sky, and the third **Pair Of Dice** was thrown by the fourth **Hand** as he reached the **Stop Sign**, holding the second **Baseball**.

Example 18: Password Length = 21 characters
Password: 566865003982021271181
Peg Words: 5-6-6-8-6-5-0-0-3-9-8-2-0-2-1-2-7-1-1-8-1

first Hand	first Ant
second Ant	first Stop Sign
third Ant	second Hand
first Vacuum	second Vacuum
Pitchfork	Baseball
second Stop Sign	first Pair Of Dice
third Vacuum	second Pair Of Dice
first Universe	third Pair Of Dice
Rainbow	second Universe
third Universe	third Stop Sign
fourth Universe	

Sentence(s):
The first **Hand** picked the first **Ant**, the second **Ant** was walking on the first **Stop Sign**, the third **Ant** bit the second **Hand**, the first **Vacuum** cleaner and the second **Vacuum** cleaner were standing near the **Pitchfork**, the **Baseball** hit the second **Stop Sign** as the first **Pair Of Dice** was cast close to the third **Vacuum** cleaner which was lying on the floor.

He threw the second **Pair Of Dice** and looked at the first **Universe**, he cast the third **Pair Of Dice** as the **Rainbow** appeared in the second **Universe** and the third **Universe**, he stopped at the third **Stop Sign** and looked at the fourth **Universe**.

Example 19:   Password Length = 22
Password: 7947765790972402383392
Peg Words: 7-9-4-7-7-6-5-7-9-0-9-7-2-4-0-2-3-8-3-3-9-2

first Rainbow	first Baseball
first Dog	second Rainbow
third Rainbow	Ant
Hand	fourth Rainbow
second Baseball	first Vacuum
third Baseball	fifth Rainbow
first Pair Of Dice	second Dog
second Vacuum	second Pair Of Dice
first Pitchfork	Stop Sign
second Pitchfork	third Pitchfork
fourth Baseball	third Pair Of Dice

Sentence(s):

The first **Rainbow** appeared as the first **Baseball** was thrown at the first **Dog**, the second **Rainbow** and the third **Rainbow** appeared as the **Ant** walked on the man's **Hand**, the fourth **Rainbow** appeared as the second **Baseball** was hurled against the door of the first **Vacuum** chamber, and the third **Baseball** was thrown as the fifth **Rainbow** appeared in the sky.

The first **Pair Of Dice** was thrown as the second **Dog**, sitting in front of the second **Vacuum** chamber, looked on, the second **Pair Of Dice** was cast where the first **Pitchfork** was lying in front of the **Stop Sign**, the second **Pitchfork** and the third **Pitchfork** were thrown at the fourth **Baseball** which was on the floor near the third **Pair Of Dice**.

Example 20:   Password Length = 23
Password: 04960721473362101403152
Peg Words: 0-4-9-6-0-7-2-1-4-7-3-3-6-2-10-1-4-0-3-1-5-2

first Vacuum	first Dog

Baseball	first Ant
second Vacuum	first Rainbow
first Pair Of Dice	first Universe
second Dog	second Rainbow
first Pitchfork	second Pitchfork
second Ant	second Pair Of Dice
Dime	second Universe
third Dog	third Vacuum
third Pitchfork	third Universe
Hand	third Pair Of Dice

Sentence(s):

He stood in front of the first **Vacuum** chamber and whistled to the first **Dog**, the **Baseball** rolled over the first **Ant**, he opened the door of the second **Vacuum** chamber when the first **Rainbow** appeared, he threw the first **Pair Of Dice** as he looked at the first **Universe**, the second **Dog** looked at the second **Rainbow**, and he threw the first **Pitchfork** and the second **Pitchfork** into the barn. The second **Ant** walked towards the second **Pair Of Dice** and the **Dime** on the table, he watched the second **Universe** as the third **Dog** ran towards the third **Vacuum** chamber, he pointed the third **Pitchfork** at the third **Universe**, and he used his **Hand** to pick the third **Pair Of Dice** from the floor.

Example 21:   Password Length = 24
Password: 146353390980788743077416
Peg Words: 1-4-6-3-5-3-3-9-0-9-8-0-7-8-8-7-4-3-0-7-7-4-1-6

first Universe	first Dog
first Ant	first Pitchfork
Hand	second Pitchfork
third Pitchfork	first Baseball
first Vacuum	second Baseball
first Stop Sign	second Vacuum

first Rainbow	second Stop Sign
third Stop Sign	second Rainbow
second Dog	fourth Pitchfork
third Vacuum	third Rainbow
fourth Rainbow	third Dog
second Universe	second Ant

Sentence(s):

He looked at the first **Universe**, the first **Dog** and first **Ant** with the first **Pitchfork** in his **Hand**, the second **Pitchfork** and the third **Pitchfork** were lying on the ground as he threw the first **Baseball** at the door of the first **Vacuum** chamber, the second **Baseball** was thrown at the first **Stop Sign**, close to the second **Vacuum** chamber.

He looked at the first **Rainbow** when he reached the second **Stop Sign** and the third **Stop Sign**, the second **Rainbow** appeared when the second **Dog** ran towards the fourth **Pitchfork**, he reached the third **Vacuum** chamber as the third **Rainbow** and the fourth **Rainbow** appeared, and the third **Dog** looked at the second **Universe** and the second **Ant**.

Example 22: Password Length = 25
Password: 5132871131326421406320777
Peg Words: 5-1-3-2-8-7-1-1-3-1-3-2-6-4-2-1-4-0-6-3-2-0-7-7-7

Hand	first Universe
first Pitchfork	first Pair Of Dice
Stop Sign	first Rainbow
second Universe	third Universe
second Pitchfork	fourth Universe
third Pitchfork	second Pair Of Dice
first Ant	first Dog
third Pair Of Dice	fifth Universe
second Dog	first Vacuum

second Ant	fourth Pitchfork
fourth Pair Of Dice	second Vacuum
second Rainbow	third Rainbow
fourth Rainbow	

Sentence(s):

He pointed his **Hand** at the first **Universe**, took the first **Pitchfork** and threw the first **Pair Of Dice** when he reached the **Stop Sign**, the first **Rainbow** appeared in the second **Universe** and the third **Universe**, he took the second **Pitchfork**, looked at the fourth **Universe**, took the third **Pitchfork** and cast the second **Pair Of Dice** as the first **Ant** and first **Dog** passed by.

He threw the third **Pair Of Dice** as he watched the fifth **Universe**, the second **Dog** was standing in front of the first **Vacuum** chamber, the second **Ant** was walking on the fourth **Pitchfork**, the fourth **Pair Of Dice** was cast in front of the door of the second **Vacuum** chamber as the second **Rainbow**, the third **Rainbow** and fourth **Rainbow** appeared in the sky.

4.2 Number-Object Practice Exercises

Exercises 1: Password Length = 4 characters

5572
7937
2782
3001
6066
8846
8684
3596
2758
6604

Exercises 2: Password Length = 5 characters

73236

88590
74939
00517
94740
03848
23572
08854
98481
50571

Exercises 3:   Password Length = 6 characters
030643
685152
888653
222503
338427
875227
629819
579465
074940
762567

Exercises 4:   Password Length = 7 characters
4864415
9671953
6832048
9462846
7985366
3675130
4719638
1474233
6075033
6274573

Exercises 5:   Password Length = 8 characters
94674379

03916880
62920304
09003695
59210459
27991497
93278951
78166285
06145021
21698561

Exercises 6:   Password Length = 9 characters

676912875
978405290
504229391
287709113
462869536
416428927
949851910
400453867
590197860
744889048

Exercises 7:   Password Length = 10 characters

9012142920
6137466911
2394296357
6498331539
6778343482
7953817828
8303557018
2323827413
4329357982
0976631617

Exercises 8:   Password Length = 11 characters

69058403261

94632580271
28919093226
70756967863
73372288816
71808543091
79528465773
03382998162
62879889137
09137008766

Exercises 9:   Password Length = 12 characters
792198552303
606811317217
010480193007
941894591984
380383001154
989810826682
985330014292
103413548444
571371859378
019222555695

Exercises 10:   Password Length = 13 characters
7468460700640
0099525569021
2527793744040
9836990567075
1847624290713
6165908727731
9728195416202
6614585826706
9215003660271
3560895292991

Exercises 11:   Password Length = 14 characters
85610477490031

59274593588876
18274577070006
18383378189261
69499667964858
22951321814168
78097543135262
64999214570164
21237318403864
75352382920343

Exercises 12:   Password Length = 15 characters
544205607475044
436354234578532
956464979221627
277319068835544
122093856694415
738801271901077
046854473071837
494871928964432
585175259692703
704656179707195

Exercises 13:   Password Length = 16 characters
0571607590155826
3470400449343928
0123501224605646
3862622577583235
7094704040722549
2373218807053553
6882806539973914
1930381759806133
1591323581834654
7592114436413048

Exercises 14:   Password Length = 17 characters
02489904748826531

71359124165957734
53529746177979041
17496011187822032
67752220844797417
61082129834579533
18007819729604267
91615639658710747
69472555595437705
67706268655424296

Exercises 15:   Password Length = 18 characters
374658647175986925
037892002619842017
991043662478288916
383496284226951042
857670531409681285
352071405260167783
787733464002429498
076985193370260836
208372276111872833
460778009499192813

Exercises 16:   Password Length = 19 characters
1826385292111684202
0151507631277262993
3634376060646488569
9851278716639664716
5884984544298535669
5423975018167724001
5469184120891890389
9837175589699301805
2347223724099762901
9646758902377489372

Exercises 17:   Password Length = 20 characters
18695958267069592864

07719187573786880731
23981944213063834757
70609973910317796293
27569707661515910249
06948993978424470034
67352855506037587510
61581177528347002811
97636822397006165731
02009396004977086061

Exercises 18:   Password Length = 21 characters
531503261891481191811
373659083873409584663
005481198600197285177
012176867526131983635
995485597438341440915
335651353061931163656
904816426025765739295
596408524617566157256
127045025878118062028
950112485754910657820

Exercises 19:   Password Length = 22 characters
3788332154059616528458
2921802015174768172637
1210705652403633259165
1702504532198979306344
3013480492309601331407
0778396800798486593344
8700093260726245290462
1352514875790841796574
9801838682965527656023
6928878105023532342023

Exercises 20:   Password Length = 23 characters
01768591903047627385426

33532051780444111058766
59529190206563803585342
13098930911447254117833
06208372389862885889595
75186054483824460659670
72987619918624451583155
89380302771250530727455
27661642420418496387703
11977684287011704532858

Exercises 21: Password Length = 24 characters
644527294446240417114774
370788328504929393476179
015822899616692046420753
59555725905954978763881
013457860916037570570005
468025272311978643695305
389791364356209195145335
999293559197228630288604
029592703258973555781028
815762283030422310682027

Exercises 22: Password Length = 25 characters
3881281998357660471582582
5389521818837945650732410
6059019130609205010090770
3819769133576782715479296
0274500829000583430693022
3173338624070874281681776
9011593380436014148672631
3864755349725991571857922
0005817172311832456706144
0675954436450146399326213

Chapter 5

Number, Alphabet and Special Character Rhyme Peg Systems

The **Special Characters** are a selection of punctuation characters that are present on standard US keyboard and frequently used in passwords. However, various operating systems and applications may apply limitations to this list of special characters presented below.

We are going to look for rhymes or near-rhymes for these special characters. These will be the peg words we will use in the recall process.

Table 5.1 Special Characters and Peg Words

Special Character	Name	Peg Word
	Space	Base
!	Exclamation	Vacillation
"	Double Quote	Noble's Coat
#	Number Sign (Hash)	Lumber
$	Dollar Sign	Brawler
%	Percent	Descent
&	Ampersand	Undersigned
'	Single Quote	Singing Goat
(	Left Parenthesis	Best Epenthesis
)	Right Parenthesis	Trite Epenthesis
*	Asterisk	Maverick
+	Plus	Truss
,	Comma	Trauma

-	Minus	Nighness
.	Full Stop	Rooftop
/	Slash	Clash
:	Colon	Stolon
;	Semicolon	Mesocolon
<	Less Than	Dress Van
=	Equal Sign	Sequel
>	Greater Than	Grader Ban
?	Question Mark	Haitian Narc
@	At Sign	Arcsine
[	Left Bracket	Felt Jacket
\	Backslash	Backlash
]	Right Bracket	Bright Racquet
^	Caret	Carrot
_	Underscore	Albacore
`	Grave Accent (Backtick)	Brave Ascent
{	Left Brace	Cleft's Place
|	Vertical Bar	Surgical Garb
}	Right Brace	Rat Race
~	Tilde	Hilde

We are going to use the rhymes or near-rhymes listed above to help code and memorize the passwords containing numbers, alphabets and special characters.

We are going to use the following rhymes and near-rhymes as peg words for the numbers: 0-9:

Table 5.2 Numbers and Peg Words

Number	Peg Word
0	Hero
1	Hun
2	Shoe

3	Tree
4	Door
5	Hive
6	Hicks
7	Heaven
8	Gate
9	Mine

For the alphabets, we use the following rhymes or near-rhymes. For each alphabet, we have a capital letter and a small letter. In order to get peg words for the small letters, we will add a qualifying adjective indicating a reduction, decrease or diminution to the peg words representing the capital letters.

I have decided here to add the word, "Little", to all the peg words for the capital letters, to represent the small letters of the alphabet.

Alphabet Rhymes / Near-Rhymes

Table 5.3 Alphabet Rhymes / Near-Rhymes

Capital Letter	Peg Word	Small Letter	Peg Word
A	Hay	a	Little Hay
B	Bee	b	Little Bee
C	Sea	c	Little Sea
D	Deal	d	Little Deal
E	Eel	e	Little Eel
F	Elf	f	Little Elf
G	Gin	g	Little Gin
H	Age	h	Little Age

I	Eye	i	Little Eye
J	Jay	j	Little Jay
K	Quay	k	Little Quay
L	Hell	ℓ	Little Hell
M	Hem	m	Little Hem
N	Hen	n	Little Hen
Ө	Hole	o	Little Hole
P	Pea	p	Little Pea
Q	Cue	q	Little Cue
R	Arc	r	Little Arc
S	Hearse	s	Little Hearse
T	Tea	t	Little Tea
U	New	u	Little New
V	Veal	v	Little Veal
W	Troubled Youth	w	Little Troubled Youth
X	Eggs	x	Little Eggs
Y	Wile	y	Little Wile
Z	Zeal	z	Little Zeal

We then code and memorize these passwords, using the peg words we have listed above.

You can use spaces in passwords but I am really not enthused about that. For the sake of illustration, I am going to use spaces in the following example:

8F 3# %q

We therefore have the following peg words:

Gate	Elf
First Base	Tree
Lumber	Second Base
Descent	Little Cue

The **Gate** has become the permanent perch of the **Elf**, in front of the **First Base**, a huge **Tree** was felled to produce **Lumber** to construct the barn, and the **Second Base** led to a steep **Descent** on the south side of the hill, and the Viceroy did not provide even a **Little Cue** to help unravel the murder of the monarch.

Numbers and Alphabets

Learning Procedure

1. You memorize the numbers and alphabets and their associated peg words. Memorize them very well through repetition and reinforcement because you will always have to remember them in order to recall the passwords.
2. You find the peg words for the numbers and alphabets in the password and arrange them in the order in which they appear in the password.
3. You construct sentences with the peg words in order to chain or link them sequentially and coherently together. The more outrageous a sentence is, the easier it is for you to remember it.
4. You memorize the sentences in order to get the correct positions of the peg words in the sentences with absolute ease.
5. You will then be able to remember the password if you remember the numbers, alphabets and their associated peg words.

How to Memorize the Sentences Constructed with the Peg Words

You will use repetition and reinforcement to learn these sentences.

1. Read the sentences inaudibly five or ten times.
2. Read the sentences audibly five or ten times.
3. Write down the sentences five or ten times.

Please continue this process till you can easily remember the sentences.

Please note that we have used the uppercase for initial letters of specific words or specific words in the groups of words in the sentences constructed in this book and bolded them only for emphasis and clarity. We crave your indulgence if you are unhappy that this may be an irremissible infraction of the rules of grammar.

5.1 Number-Alphabet Examples

Example 1:   Password Length = 4 characters
Password: 1Aℓ3

Peg Words: 1-A-ℓ-3

Hun	Hay
Little Hell	Tree

Sentence(s):
The **Hun** took **Hay** to the **Little Hell** and sat on the **Tree** there.

Example 2:   Password Length = 5 characters
Password: 4a6M9
Peg Words: 4-a-6-M-9

Door	Little Hay

Hicks   Hem
Mine

Sentence(s):

He went through the **Door** and took a **Little Hay**, and sent it to the **Hicks**, who were mending the **Hem** of the dress of the girl in the **Mine**.

Example 3:   Password Length = 6 characters
Password: 2B6mU1
Peg Words: 2-B-6-m-U-1

Shoe	Bee
Hicks	Little Hem
New	Hun

Sentence(s):

The **Shoe** has become the hiding place for the **Bee**, the **Hicks** told her to repair the **Little Hem** of the toy's dress, which appeared to be quite **New** but which the **Hun** disliked.

Example 4:   Password Length = 7 characters
Password: 3b3N9u2
Peg Words: 3-b-3-N-9-u-2

first Tree	Little Bee
second Tree	Hen
Mine	Little New
Shoe	

Sentence(s):

The first **Tree** was the resting place of the **Little Bee**, and the second **Tree** was the roosting place of the **Hen**, and he went to the **Mine** with a shirt which was a **Little New** and the **Shoe** he had recently bought.

Example 5:   Password Length = 8 characters
Password: 40C4n8V9
Peg Words: 4-0-C-4-n-8-V-9

first Door	Hero
Sea	second Door
Little Hen	Gate
Veal	Mine

Sentence(s):

He went through the first **Door** to the villa of the **Hero**, which was close to the **Sea**, the second **Door** led to the coop of the **Little Hen**, and he passed through the **Gate** to get some **Veal** before going to the **Mine**.

Example 6:   Password Length = 9 characters
Password: 7c706v9E3
Peg Words: 7-c-7-0-6-v-9-E-3

first Heaven	Little Sea
second Heaven	Hole
Hicks	Little Veal
Mine	Eel
Tree	

Sentence(s):

The first **Heaven** had a **Little Sea**, the second **Heaven** was in the black **Hole**, the **Hicks** got a **Little Veal** and went straight to the **Mine**, and the **Eel** was hanging from a branch of the **Tree**.

Example 7:   Password Length = 10 characters
Password: 8D1o73X8e1
Peg Words: 8-D-1-o-7-3-X-8-e-1

first Gate	Deal
Hun	Little Hole
Heaven	Tree

| Eggs | second Gate |
| Little Eel | Hun |

Sentence(s):

He passed through the first **Gate** and got the **Deal** with the **Hun**, and then went through the **Little Hole** to **Heaven** where he saw the **Tree** bearing the nest full of **Eggs**, and then moved to the second **Gate** which led to the **Little Eel** caught by the **Hun**.

Example 8:   Password Length = 11 characters

Password: 4d5P4x2F9n6

Peg Words: 4-d-5-P-4-x-2-F-9-n-6

first Door	Little Deal
Hive	Pea
second Door	Little Eggs
Shoe	Elf
Mine	Little Hen
Hicks	

Sentence(s):

The first **Door** led to the room where they met to make that **Little Deal**, in the **Hive** was the **Pea**, the second **Door** led to the **Little Eggs** and the **Shoe** of the **Elf**, and the **Mine** was now the coop of the **Little Hen** which belonged to the **Hicks**.

Example 9:   Password Length = 12 characters

Password: 8E6p5Y05f306

Peg Words: 8-E-6-p-5-Y-0-5-f-3-0-6

Gate	Eel
first Hicks	Little Pea
first Hive	Wile
Hero	second Hive
Little Elf	Tree
Hole	second Hicks

Sentence(s):

He passed through the **Gate** and went to the kitchen, where the **Eel** had been placed on the table, the first group of **Hicks** placed the **Little Pea** in the first **Hive**, the **Wile** of the **Hero** could help him buy the second **Hive** at a much cheaper price, the **Little Elf** was sitting on the **Tree**, and the **Hole** being dug by the second group of **Hicks** has become bigger and deeper.

Example 10: Password Length = 13 characters
Password: 3e3Q7y20G68o2
Peg Words: 3e3Q7y20G68o2

first Tree	Little Eel
second Tree	Cue
Heaven	Little Wile
first Shoe	Hero
Gin	Hicks
Gate	Little Hole
second Shoe	

Sentence(s):

He passed the first **Tree** and saw the **Little Eel** on the second **Tree**, he took a **Cue** from the story he had heard about **Heaven**, he used a **Little Wile** to get the first **Shoe** from the **Hero**, who had drunk so much **Gin** that he was helplessly intoxicated, and the **Hicks** went through the **Gate** and looked inside the **Little Hole** dug in the garden and found the second **Shoe**.

Example 11: Password Length = 14 characters
Password: 8F4q8Z7g45P5s6
Peg Words: 8F4q8Z7g45P5s6

first Gate	Elf
first Door	Little Cue
second Gate	Zeal

Heaven	Little Gin
second Door	first Hive
Pea	second Hive
Little Hearse	Hicks

Sentence(s):

He passed through the first **Gate** and saw the **Elf** relaxing on the couch, he then went through the first **Door**, with a **Little Cue** as to what was going to happen, he passed through the second **Gate** with the **Zeal** to go to **Heaven**, he drank a **Little Gin**, went through the second **Door** and got to the first **Hive**, he put the **Pea** in the second **Hive**, and then saw the **Little Hearse** being pushed down the lane by the **Hicks**.

Example 12:   Password Length = 15 characters
Password: 2f3R4z58H0p80T3
Peg Words: 2-f-3-R-4-z-5-8-H-0-p-8-0-T-3

Shoe	Little Elf
first Tree	Arc
Door	Little Zeal
Hive	first Gate
Age	first Hero
Little Pea	second Gate
second Hero	Tea
second Tree	

Sentence(s):

The **Shoe** of the **Little Elf** was caught up on a branch in the first **Tree**, when it was thrown in an **Arc** through the **Door** with **Little Zeal**, the **Hive** was taken through the first **Gate**, the **Age** of the first **Hero** was unknown, he took the **Little Pea**, and then passed through the second **Gate** and gave it to the second **Hero**, who was drinking **Tea** under the second **Tree**.

Example 13:   Password Length = 16 characters
Password: 9G8r5A7h78Q0t2Z8
Peg Words: 9-G-8-r-5-A-7-h-7-8-Q-0-t-2-Z-8

Mine	Gin
first Gate	Little Arc
Hive	Hay
first Heaven	Little Age
second Heaven	second Gate
Cue	Hero
Little Tea	Shoe
Zeal	third Gate

Sentence(s):

Before he went to the **Mine**, he drank a **Little Gin**, passed through the first **Gate** and saw a **Little Arc** drawn on the pillar of the house, he took the **Hive** and placed it gently on the **Hay** in the barn, the first **Heaven** was older when compared with the **Little Age** of the second **Heaven**, he passed through the second **Gate**, and taking a **Cue** from the **Hero**, he drank a **Little Tea**, took the **Shoe** with **Zeal** and went strutting through the third **Gate**.

Example 14:   Password Length = 17 characters
Password: 1g5S4a72I6q36U5z6
Peg Words: 1-g-5-S-4-a-7-2-I-6-q-3-6-U-5-z-6

Hun	Little Gin
first Hive	Hearse
Door	Little Hay
Heaven	Shoe
Eye	first Hicks
Little Cue	Tree
second Hicks	New
second Hive	Little Zeal
third Hicks	

Sentence(s):

The **Hun** drank a **Little Gin**, took the first **Hive** and put it in the **Hearse**, he passed through the **Door**, took a **Little Hay** and went to **Heaven** with the **Shoe**, he caught the **Eye** of the first group of **Hicks**, who had a **Little Cue** as to what at all on the **Tree** the second group of **Hicks** was interested in, and he was **New** in the area, but he moved towards the second **Hive**, but he however had **Little Zeal** to give it to the third group of **Hicks**.

Example 15:   Password Length = 18 characters
Password: 6H1s5B80i30R10u5A6
Peg Words: 6-H-1-s-5-B-8-0-i-3-0-R-1-0-u-5-A-6

first Hicks	Age
first Hun	Little Hearse
first Hive	Bee
Gate	first Hero
Little Eye	Tree
second Hero	Arc
second Hun	third Hero
Little New	second Hive
Hay	second Hicks

Sentence(s):

The first group of **Hicks** tried to guess the **Age** of the first **Hun** who was driving the **Little Hearse**, the first **Hive** was where the **Bee** came from and passed through the **Gate** and stung the first **Hero**, the **Little Eye** in the bark of the **Tree** resembled that of the second **Hero**, it was an **Arc** through which the second **Hun** flew through the air and landed on the third **Hero,** who was standing by his **Little New** but expensive car, and the second **Hive** was placed on the **Hay** the second group of **Hicks** was piling up.

Example 16:   Password Length = 19 characters
Password: 5h1T6b8Jr3V29a5G6k3
Peg Words: 5-h-1-T-6-b-8-J-r-3-V-2-9-a-5-G-6-k-3

first Hive	Little Age
Hun	Tea
first Hicks	Little Bee
Gate	Jay
Little Arc	first Tree
Veal	Shoe
Mine	Little Hay
second Hive	Gin
second Hicks	Little Quay
second Tree	

Sentence(s):

He took the first **Hive** with a **Little Age** and sent it to the **Hun** who was drinking **Tea**, the first group of **Hicks** caught the **Little Bee**, then passed through the **Gate** and saw the **Jay** flying in a **Little Arc** over the first **Tree**, he ate the roasted **Veal**, took the **Shoe** and went to the **Mine**, he spread a **Little Hay** on the second **Hive**, then gave some **Gin** to the second group of **Hicks** standing on the **Little Quay**, and then went to the second **Tree** to pluck some fruits.

Example 17:   Password Length = 20 characters
Password: 8l4t1F6j3P2v30B4g5L9
Peg Words: 8-l-4-t-1-F-6-j-3-P-2-v-3-0-B-4-g-5-L-9

Gate	Eye
first Door	Little Tea
Hun	Elf
Hicks	Little Jay
first Tree	Pea
Shoe	Little Veal

second Tree	Hero
Bee	second Door
Little Gin	Hive
Hell	Mine

Sentence(s):

He went through the **Gate** and saw the **Eye** painted on the first **Door**, the **Little Tea** the **Hun** gave to the **Elf** made him agree to go and deliver the message to the **Hicks**, the **Little Jay** flew to the first **Tree**, then zoomed down to try and pick the **Pea** from the ground, he took the **Shoe**, ate a **Little Veal** and went to the second **Tree**, where the **Hero** was standing and looking at the **Bee** buzzing around in the shade, and he passed through the second **Door**, drank a **Little Gin**, took the **Hive** to **Hell** and came back to doze in the **Mine**.

Example 18:   Password Length = 21 characters

Password: 0i7U9f5K1p60W8b54H9ℓ7

Peg Words: 0-i-7-U-9-f-5-K-1-p-6-0-W-8-b-5-4-H-9-ℓ-7

first Hero	Little Eye
first Heaven	New
first Mine	Little Elf
first Hive	Quay
Hun	Little Pea
Hicks	second Hero
Troubled Youth	Gate
Little Bee	second Hive
Door	Age
second Mine	Little Hell
second Heaven	

Sentence(s):

He watched the first **Hero** with his **Little Eye** going into the first **Heaven**, he took the **New** equipment for the first **Mine** to the

Little Elf sitting in front of the first **Hive**, and when he got to the **Quay**, he saw the **Hun** giving the **Little Pea** to the **Hicks**.

The second **Hero** advised the **Troubled Youth** to stay away from the **Gate**, leading to where the **Little Bee** was buzzing around in front of the second **Hive**, he passed through the **Door** and asked the **Age** of the owner of the second **Mine**, and went to **Little Hell** before continuing to the second **Heaven**.

Example 19:   Password Length = 22 characters

Password: 9J2u5G1k9Q22w16C89h7M8

Peg Words: 9-J-2-u-5-G-1-k-9-Q-2-2-w-1-6-C-8-9-h-7-M-8

first Mine	Jay
first Shoe	Little New
Hive	Gin
first Hun	Little Quay
second Mine	Cue
second Shoe	third Shoe
Little Troubled Youth	second Hun
Hicks	Sea
first Gate	third Mine
Little Age	Heaven
Hem	second Gate

Sentence(s):

When he came out of the first **Mine**, he saw the **Jay** flying about, the first **Shoe** which was a **Little New** was in front of the **Hive**, he drank some **Gin** and then went to the first **Hun**, who was standing on the **Little Quay**, and he then went to the second **Mine** without any **Cue** as to where to find the second **Shoe** and the third **Shoe**. The **Little Troubled Youth** reported the second **Hun** to the **Hicks** who had gone to **Sea**, he passed through the first **Gate** and went to the third **Mine** which is of a **Little Age** that could not be compared to that of **Heaven,** and he adjusted the **Hem** of his daughter's dress before going through the second **Gate.**

Example 20: Password Length = 23 characters
Password: 8j5V6g1L43q75X08c5l3m00

Peg Words: 8-j-5-V-6-g-1-L-4-3-q-7-5-X-0-8-c-5-l-3-m-0-0

first Gate	Little Jay
first Hive	Veal
Hicks	Little Gin
Hun	Hell
Door	first Tree
Little Cue	Heaven
second Hive	Eggs
first Hero	second Gate
Little Sea	third Hive
Eye	second Tree
Little Hem	Hole
second Hero	

Sentence(s):

He passed through the first **Gate** and looked at the **Little Jay** flying around the first **Hive,** the **Veal** eaten by the **Hicks** with a **Little Gin** was given to them by the **Hun** who has gone to **Hell,** and he went through the **Door** to the first **Tree** with a **Little Cue** as to how he could go to **Heaven.**

The second **Hive** was holding the **Eggs,** the first **Hero** passed through the second **Gate** and went to the **Little Sea** carrying the third **Hive,** he caught the **Eye** of the lady as he reached the second **Tree,** and the lady was mending the **Little Hem** and the **Hole** in her dress before meeting the second **Hero.**

Example 21: Password Length = 24 characters
Password: 1K8v9H60l2R46x9D48i2N9o2

Peg Words: 1-K-8-v-9-H-6-0-ℓ-2-R-4-6-x-9-D-4-8-i-2-N-9-o-2

Hun	Quay
first Gate	Little Veal
first Mine	Age
first Hicks	Hero
Little Hell	first Shoe
Arc	first Door
second Hicks	Little Eggs
second Mine	Deal
second Door	second Gate
Little Eye	second Shoe
Hen	third Mine
Little Hole	third Shoe

Sentence(s):

The **Hun** stood on the **Quay** for some time before passing through the first **Gate**, he ate a **Little Veal** and went to the first **Mine**, the **Age** of one of the people in the first group of **Hicks** who was a **Hero** was never known, and when he left the **Little Hell**, he threw the first **Shoe** in an **Arc** through the first **Door** into the hall. The second group of **Hicks** sent the **Little Eggs** to the second **Mine** when a **Deal** was reached with the owner, he passed through the second **Door** and the second **Gate** and saw the **Little Eye** painted on the wall, and then took the second **Shoe**, and he took the **Hen** to the third **Mine**, and in a **Little Hole**, he found the third **Shoe**.

Example 22: Password Length = 25 characters
Password: 6kW0h04M25r71Y85d54J1n7P3
Peg Words: 6-k-W-0-h-0-4-M-2-5-r-7-1-Y-8-5-d-5-4-J-1-n-7-P-3

Hicks	Little Quay
Troubled Youth	first Hero
Little Age	second Hero
first Door	Hem

Shoe	first Hive
Little Arc	first Heaven
first Hun	Wile
Gate	second Hive
Little Deal	third Hive
second Door	Jay
second Hun	Little Hen
second Heaven	Pea
Tree	

Sentence(s):

The **Hicks** were standing on the **Little Quay** talking to the **Troubled Youth**, the first **Hero** was commenting on the **Little Age** of the second **Hero** who passed through the first **Door**, he sewed the **Hem** of the dress, and took the **Shoe** and the first **Hive** on which a **Little Arc** was painted and went to the first **Heaven**.

The first **Hun** displayed an uncanny **Wile** as he lied his way through the **Gate** and reached the second **Hive**, where he had a **Little Deal** with regard to the purchase of the third **Hive**, he passed through the second **Door**, saw the **Jay** flying about, and the second **Hun** holding the **Little Hen** and went to the second **Heaven**, and took the **Pea** from the **Tree**.

5.2 Number-Alphabet Practice Exercises

Exercises 1:   Password Length = 4 characters

9jE2
1Ke8
3kF5
7Lf1
0l4ℓG

6Mg0
5mH9
9Nh6

4nl1
60i7

Exercises 2: Password Length = 5 characters
1S1a9
54sB3
26Tb7
5t3C8
3c6U8
7D1u6
8Vd51
25vE1
9W4e2
1w2F2

Exercises 3: Password Length = 6 characters
2x0dM9
14YEm5
5y8Ne9
9Z5nF0
8fO8z1
9AGo80
44aPg0
7B5pH2
1Q0bh3
8Cl7q9

Exercises 4: Password Length = 7 characters
3H7s1F0
04f5Th6
21G2tl3
4i7U0g6
5H9J2u3
79j9hV0

4KI6v79
78Xi7k6
4J1x8L4
3Y7j5ℓ6

Exercises 5:   Password Length = 8 characters
4a2J95q7
38j9BR49
3b37K4r6
1kC13S05
2L67c3s8
89DT76ℓ2
3t70M2d9
78U5E1m0
4u9N85e9
58F2V9n6

Exercises 6:   Password Length = 9 characters
1gM8z67P5
9p14m5HA6
9h6a3N6Q7
7n3qI54B2
2i8b3O7R2
4o6r9C5J7
8jP2c18S4
8D6s5p4K8
1d7U0k5T3
0EL76t3u8

Exercises 7:   Password Length = 10 characters
2U5c03H5x9
6D23u1hY29

95l7d3V4y8

3E80i7Z6v0

4W16J2e1z5

6A2F6j7w28

4K6a8X31f9

9x6B5k8G38

36g52YL1b3

5y1C9l78l3

Exercises 8: Password Length = 11 characters

5a4V6f0M3R7

7r9m3B5v8G6

2S6b4W3N1g7

7w61n9C4Hs8

4c1h706X9T8

4t8xl73o6D5

9U8d4P7Y8i6

25y9J3uE8p7

3Q5j8e3Z4V5

4F9v3z7q2K6

Exercises 9: Password Length = 12 characters

7C85M04A10t3

2m31o0c9U8a6

7B0u9D8P43N2

4p0n9b34d8V6

3v4C1EQ95087

4e5o8c7qW169

4D9w8R20F7P6

4p3Xd078r5f6

0SGx7E284Q63

7Y9s06g2e4q8

Exercises 10:   Password Length = 13 characters

0a897p5m6E0J3
9j18N4Q36e7B0
56b3K6n9F5q72
35C9k79R508f4
03L4r5G6o9c10
8P0Sg7D456092
8M9s09H46d4p2
5E75m2T9Q8h31
6N8q91e697lt3
3i7U8FR0n1354

Exercises 11:   Password Length = 14 characters

7XC63g5aK93s24
97c8T6H0B2x4k5
4t5Y60g3b5c1hL3
1y8CH9U6dl20863
6h7M5c1E6u4Z0i6
7D8z3l5J2V4m1e9
9A15i78dN2v3F5
3WE8j5n9J0a6f83
5e2B460Gj78K6w0
3o4X92bk14F8g0

Exercises 12:   Password Length = 15 characters

1B2e85m7t62l8Q4
8q517ib3F8N9U27
3C81u4f9n7R4J83
1V3G7r508c906j4
9g15o3K62D4Sv76
8s9H24P8X7d5k30

6p1L84E2T73h9x1

3I9t14l5Y63Q7e8

8M5q60F4U5i96y7

6R9Z2u14J05m7f8

Exercises 13:   Password Length = 16 characters

6u4X5a1g0J7n31R8

4H9r081B60j7Vx8

74K0v1Y8h9o7S0b3

53Py1s24W6C8l9k7

8i703L6Z8p71wTc4

0l3X7t0D8Q3J6z80

64j78d9AU6M4q3x5

6m9Y7a8R3E5K6u40

5V40e3k2r8y1N7B6

4S3b6n5Z7L08v7F9

Exercises 14:   Password Length = 17 characters

4D8k93g8Pt46J3W18

5j2w34LU9d8p15H07

3h7u8K19E64l0X4Q2

5q8lV6x4k341e79M5

0m9v6FL1Y98i27R40

0J8y6r04W3N5f89l4

8n65M2j4S3Z62Gw19

9g20s4X050K17m9z2

5L16N7H1x3T9o8A76

2n37P1t4a6h98l5Y7

Exercises 15:   Password Length = 18 characters

63m1s4l09f5z247C8

2i36A1c09G8T50N13

62n32D06g0J49a2t3
1B4d3H9j5U85O2976
3h4u0K31o9E82b465
857e4C43k9V67I8P0
4L3p75i96c18F24v6
3D45f6W17ℓ49J8Q50
47w2j61q03d2G4M80
2m6R034E75X6K89g3

Exercises 16:   Password Length = 19 characters
8B0u6i75L3p1d49R7G2
5r97Vg6E5b4J36ℓ91Q8
50C2v3M4j04q9H6e7S8
8R42K6Fm1W207h5s3c9
5N6w9D8r5I4k2T13f07
70L32t1G8S7i5d2X4n6
8g27E5O6U4ℓ3x8s4J09
41T5j3Y2u7oI54e5M1t8
7F8y19m3V2K1U8i40P5
3p5Z1u42J8v53O7k9f2

Exercises 17:   Password Length = 20 characters
2x62J18c0h6Vm4s8O9A6F0
8I5a3N46Y1T8vD6f57j4o6
6t2K418G2d9n5P7y4Wi5B3
4O5Z6J3b8wE6U09g10k4p8
06Q0X34z6L1u0oC7H2e4j1
9h6K05c7VP3q6F5x41A8I6
59p8I6R5Y1M2a0f3v4k0D7
0m3d1G20BW6Q7i50Ly4r26
3ℓ27E5J0q6g84SZ5b76Nw1
26n4R8zC2s9X4e2M16H7j0

Exercises 18:   Password Length = 21 characters

0Y702E95r67g9T8bK19N6

14C6S8t7y0k216n5H3e54

942F5h1009s4c8U7Z9L37

9T72D08zℓ13l021o4f5u1

76G40i3d9P7V8t3A758M9

8v631a09m5p3E42J6U5g7

6e8N53j2H17u04Q58W6B9

74K6n1w5V29q36b80F3h9

354C95f17058klOR3v6X0

4G89r3x5i0L182c6W78o3

Exercises 19:   Password Length = 22 characters

0a61f89v26M76X32l1C4k0

98x7m0c74i625W9G48L3B0

3J768w9N17b6Y8l43D6g92

087y9M05d9n60H5X8j0C17

68c71m59h47K96x208E3Z6

3k573Y2e8o90z14Dl6N924

1d320A5P7L46i8F39y46n5

1f29J83Z45ℓ93a8070E1p6

38B7o58j97G6Q30M4z65e0

4A79q2F14m08b29K50g8P1

Exercises 20:   Password Length = 23 characters

0P18b6f9T21Y86v32D9H4r7

59y3G2S71h3p08t64C2W3d8

4Q57w2E58U20Z5c9s42l6g9

25z3H5T4e9i2q647D08X6u3

8x71R050V3d7F9J5t86A7h2

9j5a82v41f96U27Y4l0E8r1

117

3e0S8G19y57i2K6W5B32u40
5J0F1k8V4w5g98s03Z45b36
2z19C6L4f08X9j5v1H73T02
7W46G50t12h03A1c8ℓ7x4K9

Exercises 21:   Password Length = 24 characters
4k56Q27V05t3Z82M9b4x19o6
8C92P3v91m4L65q19Y67U8z9
85N3R7y6A0p50u8c9ℓ064W73
02V94M2D93n94w5a6Q8Z7r90
47Ө23X46S8q4B2d8v95z4m12
1R02A6W49N8E5x047o8b4s30
59T8C03P25e7r65w20Y4n6a9
9X81B24p81c7y48Ө9t36S1F5
40s6D5U81b28o3f9x5Q12Z94
6d82P3q70z5G6u09Y8T405C2

Exercises 22:   Password Length = 25 characters
1E3t152n67C45h8W7Q62K49z0
76A3k96q5w0ℓ4c82e7Ө1U0978
38o5X0u49F62L8R17a6i58D27
8r17J56ℓ89B72V9d3P45x7f06
576M8S13Y0G5j62v49p7E8b64
2C96g0W5Q14s87m2y60K19e35
6N85T4Z0c83k24w5F9q25H176
29h7z0R4f23n187t92L16X3D8
7x6A804ℓ167U2l3d54Ө9G8r67
9u46i8S1a30g7Y18E3M45o748

118

Numbers and Special Characters

Learning Procedure

1. You memorize the numbers and special characters and their associated peg words. Memorize them very well through repetition and reinforcement because you will always have to remember them in order to recall the passwords.
2. You find the peg words for the numbers and special characters in the password and arrange them in the order in which they appear in the password.
3. You construct sentences with the peg words in order to chain or link them sequentially and coherently together. The more outrageous a sentence is, the easier it is for you to remember it.
4. You memorize the sentences in order to get the correct positions of the peg words in the sentences with absolute ease.
5. You will then be able to remember the password if you remember the numbers, special characters and their associated peg words.

How to Memorize the Sentences Constructed with the Peg Words

You will use repetition and reinforcement to learn these sentences.

1. Read the sentences inaudibly five or ten times.
2. Read the sentences audibly five or ten times.
3. Write down the sentences five or ten times.

Please continue this process till you can easily remember the sentences.

Please note that we have used the uppercase for initial letters of specific words or specific words in the groups of words in the sentences constructed in this book and bolded them only for emphasis and clarity. We crave your indulgence if you are unhappy that this may be an irremissible infraction of the rules of grammar.

5.3 Number-Special Character Examples

Example 1:   Password Length = 4 characters
Password: 5![0
Peg Words:

Hive	Vacillation
Felt Jacket	Hero

Sentence(s):
He took the **Hive** but his **Vacillation** was noticeable before he wore the **Felt Jacket** of the **Hero**.

Example 2:   Password Length = 5 characters
Password: 8"1\4
Peg Words:

Gate	Noble's Coat
Hun	Backlash
Door	

Sentence(s):
He passed through the **Gate**, wearing a **Noble's Coat**, talked to the **Hun** in relation to the **Backlash** of criticisms in the media, and then went through the **Door** to the other side of the villa.

Example 3:   Password Length = 6 characters
Password: 6#4]-8
Peg Words:

Hicks	Lumber

Door	Bright Racquet
Nighness	Gate

Sentence(s):

The **Hicks** cut the **Lumber** into pieces, then went through the **Door** to take the **Bright Racquet**, and he noticed the **Nighness** of the main **Gate** to the barn.

Example 4:   Password Length = 7 characters
Password: 7$2^3.5
Peg Words:

Heaven	Brawler
Shoe	Carrot
Tree	Rooftop
Hive	

Sentence(s):

Heaven was not a place for the **Brawler**, the **Shoe** and the **Carrot** had been placed on the **Tree**, and on the **Rooftop** was the **Hive**.

Example 5:   Password Length = 8 characters
Password: 6%7_0/!5
Peg Words:

Hicks	Descent
Heaven	Albacore
Hero	Clash
Vacillation	Hive

Sentence(s):

The **Hicks** followed his **Descent** and ascension to **Heaven**, the **Albacore** was a delicacy for the **Hero** who was involved in the **Clash** with the street fighters, and his **Vacillation** before going near the **Hive** shocked everyone.

Example 6:   Password Length = 9 characters

Password: 8&0`9:6"7

Peg Words:

Gate	Undersigned
Hero	Brave Ascent
Mine	Stolon
Hicks	Noble's Coat
Heaven	

Sentence(s):

He went through the **Gate** and met the one who **Undersigned** the contract, the **Hero** was congratulated for his **Brave Ascent** into the **Mine** on the side of the mountain, the **Stolon** from the plant was taken by one of the **Hicks**, wearing a **Noble's Coat**, and sent to **Heaven**.

Example 7:   Password Length = 10 characters
Password: 7'8{6;2#?9

Peg Words:

Heaven	Singing Goat
Gate	Cleft's Place
Hicks	Mesocolon
Shoe	Lumber
Haitian Narc	Mine

Sentence(s):

He came from **Heaven** and saw the **Singing Goat** passing through the **Gate,** and he moved to the **Cleft's Place** on the large rock in the garden, one of the **Hicks** had a problem with his **Mesocolon**, and the **Shoe** of the lumberjack, who was cutting **Lumber** on the field, was seized by the **Haitian Narc** and taken to the **Mine**.

Example 8:   Password Length = 11 characters
Password: 4(3|6<0$6@2

Peg Words:

Door	Best Epenthesis
Tree	Surgical Garb
first Hicks	Dress Van
Hero	Brawler
second Hicks	Arcsine
Shoe	

Sentence(s):

He passed through the **Door** and gave us the **Best Epenthesis** for the word, "bush", and then sat under the **Tree**, he gave the **Surgical Garb** to the first group of **Hicks**, who then went to the **Dress Van** to hang it there together with the dresses of the models, the **Hero** was able to subdue the **Brawler**, and the second group of **Hicks** was able to successfully guess the **Arcsine** of the given angle before taking the **Shoe** away.

Example 9: Password Length = 12 characters
Password: 2)3}1=58%5[0
Peg Words:

Shoe	Trite Epenthesis
Tree	Rat Race
Hun	Sequel
first Hive	Gate
Descent	second Hive
Felt Jacket	Hero

Sentence(s):

He wore the **Shoe** and thought about a **Trite Epenthesis** for the word, "church", and passed the **Tree** thinking about the **Rat Race** the **Hun** was involved in, the **Sequel** of which he could not imagine what it would be, he took the first **Hive**, went through the **Gate**, his **Descent** down the slope was risky, and he then took the second **Hive** and gave the **Felt Jacket** to the **Hero**.

Example 10:   Password Length = 13 characters
Password: 5*8~9>98&52\9
Peg Words:

first Hive	Maverick
first Gate	Hilde
first Mine	Grader Ban
second Mine	second Gate
Undersigned	second Hive
Shoe	Backlash
third Mine	

Sentence(s):

The first **Hive** was taken by the **Maverick** through the first **Gate** and given to **Hilde**, on the road from the first **Mine**, there is a **Grader Ban** for road construction to the second **Mine** and the second **Gate**, he **Undersigned** the contract to lease the second **Hive** to anyone interested, he took the **Shoe** and there was a **Backlash** of protests from the people in the third **Mine**.

Example 11:   Password Length = 14 characters
Password: 3+8!9?1'80]4%9
Peg Words:

Tree	Truss
first Gate	Vacillation
first Mine	Haitian Narc
Hun	Singing Goat
second Gate	Hero
Bright Racquet	Door
Descent	second Mine

Sentence(s):

The **Tree** was close to the **Truss** which supported the roof near the first **Gate**, he showed some **Vacillation** on his way to the first **Mine** after the **Haitian Narc** had arrested the **Hun** who possessed the cocaine, the **Singing Goat** went through the second **Gate** and met the **Hero** with the **Bright Racquet**, and he passed through the **Door** to the sharp **Descent** leading to the second **Mine**.

Example 12:   Password Length = 15 characters
Password: 2,9"5@69(30^2&9
Peg Words:

first Shoe	Trauma
first Mine	Noble's Coat
Hive	Arcsine
Hicks	second Mine
Best Epenthesis	Tree
Hero	Carrot
second Shoe	Undersigned
third Mine	

Sentence(s):

The first **Shoe** came off when he suffered a **Trauma** in the first **Mine**, he was wearing a **Noble's Coat** when he brought the **Hive** to us, the value of the **Arcsine** given by the **Hicks** who owned the second **Mine** was absolutely wrong, he gave the **Best Epenthesis** for the word, "box", under the **Tree** where the **Hero** was noisily chewing **Carrot**, and he gave the second **Shoe** to the one who **Undersigned** the sales contract for the third **Mine**.

Example 13:   Password Length = 16 characters
Password: 7-5#0[2)62_8'7;9
Peg Words:

first Heaven	Nighness

Hive	Lumber
Hero	Felt Jacket
first Shoe	Trite Epenthesis
Hicks	second Shoe
Albacore	Gate
Singing Goat	second Heaven
Mesocolon	Mine

Sentence(s):

From the first **Heaven**, he saw the **Nighness** of the **Hive** to the **Lumber** piled in the forest, the **Hero** wearing the **Felt Jacket** took the first **Shoe**, a **Trite Epenthesis** was given by the **Hicks** for the word, "buzz", he took the second **Shoe** and the **Albacore** and went through the **Gate**, he saw the **Singing Goat** entering the second **Heaven**, and he realized that he had no problem with his **Mesocolon** before he went into the **Mine**.

Example 14: Password Length = 17 characters
Password: 9.6$2\9*72`09(3<8
Pèg Words:

first Mine	Rooftop
Hicks	Brawler
first Shoe	Backlash
second Mine	Maverick
Heaven	second Shoe
Brave Ascent	Hero
third Mine	Best Epenthesis
Tree	Dress Van
Gate	

Sentence(s):

He came from the **Mine** and went to the **Rooftop** where the **Hicks** and the **Brawler** were arguing, the first **Shoe** was thrown at him as a result of the **Backlash** from the nasty statements he had made, the second **Mine** belonged to the **Maverick** who had gone to **Heaven**, he took the second **Shoe** and made the **Brave Ascent** to the top of the mountain where the **Hero** who owned the third **Mine** stood gesticulating to him, and he gave the **Best Epenthesis** for the word, "arch", under the **Tree** where the **Dress Van** for the mannequins was stationed before passing through the **Gate** and going to the trade fair.

Example 15: Password Length = 18 characters
Password: 6/3%5]61+86{36)4=7
Peg Words:

first Hicks	Clash
first Tree	Descent
Hive	Bright Racquet
second Hicks	Hun
Truss	Gate
third Hicks	Cleft's Place
second Tree	fourth Hicks
Trite Epenthesis	Door
Sequel	Heaven

Sentence(s):
The first group of **Hicks** was involved in the first **Clash**, the first **Tree** was at the top of the **Descent** which led down to the **Hive**, the **Bright Racquet** was taken by the second group of **Hicks** and given to the **Hun**, the **Truss** was placed close to the **Gate**, the third group of **Hicks** went to the **Cleft's Place** on the cliff, he went to the second **Tree** and talked to the fourth group of **Hicks** who gave a **Trite Epenthesis** for the word, "bench", and he opened the **Door** in a **Sequel** to the drama leading to **Heaven**.

Example 16: Password Length = 19 characters
Password: 0:8&2^4,01|87*2>9!6

Peg Words:

first Hero	Stolon
first Gate	Undersigned
first Shoe	Carrot
Door	Trauma
second Hero	Hun
Surgical Garb	second Gate
Heaven	Maverick
second Shoe	Grader Ban
Mine	Vacillation
Hicks	

Sentence(s):

The first **Hero** took the **Stolon** from the plant to the first **Gate**, where he saw the one who **Undersigned** the contract for the research on it, he took the first **Shoe** and the **Carrot** and went to the **Door**, the **Trauma** of the second **Hero** was seen by the **Hun** wearing the **Surgical Garb**, the second **Gate** to **Heaven** was where the **Maverick** had taken the second **Shoe**, there was a **Grader Ban** for road construction all the way to the **Mine**, and the **Vacillation** of the **Hicks** to support the worthy cause was unexpected.

Example 17: Password Length = 20 characters
Password: 1;4'3_7-68}91+42?0"5
Peg Words:

first Hun	Mesocolon
first Door	Singing Goat
Tree	Albacore
Heaven	Nighness
Hicks	Gate
Rat Race	Mine
second Hun	Truss

second Door	Shoe
Haitian Narc	Hero
Noble's Coat	Hive

Sentence(s):

The first **Hun** who had a problem with his **Mesocolon** passed through the first **Door** and saw the **Singing Goat** under the **Tree**, he enjoyed eating **Albacore** before going to **Heaven**, the **Nighness** of the **Hicks** to the whole situation disqualified their judgment of it, and he went through the **Gate** thinking about the **Rat Race** he was involved in, before heading towards the **Mine**.

The second **Hun** jumped down from the **Truss**, then passed through the second **Door** wearing the **Shoe**, before reaching the **Haitian Narc** who had arrested the **Hero**, who was wearing a **Noble's Coat** and standing in front of the **Hive**.

Example 18:   Password Length = 21 characters
Password: 7<6(4`61.32~92,45@1#8
Peg Words:

Heaven	Dress Van
first Hicks	Best Epenthesis
first Door	Brave Ascent
second Hicks	first Hun
Rooftop	Tree
first Shoe	Hilde
Mine	second Shoe
Trauma	second Door
Hive	Arcsine
second Hun	Lumber
Gate	

Sentence(s):

He came from **Heaven** and saw the **Dress Van** belonging to the first group of **Hicks**, who had provided the **Best Epenthesis** for the word, "marsh", he passed through the first **Door** and made a **Brave Ascent** to the top of the hill where the second group of **Hicks** was involved in a heated argument with the first **Hun**, and he jumped from the **Rooftop** onto the **Tree**, holding the first **Shoe**, which he gave to **Hilde**.

He left the **Mine** with the second **Shoe** and suffered a **Trauma** as he passed through the second **Door**, he then reached the **Hive**, the **Arcsine** was correctly determined by the second **Hun**, and the **Lumber** was carried through the **Gate** by horse cart.

Example 19: Password Length = 22 characters
Password: 2=8)6{12/93!46-17[51$4
Peg Words:

first Shoe	Sequel
Gate	Trite Epenthesis
first Hicks	Cleft's Place
first Hun	second Shoe
Clash	Mine
Tree	Vacillation
first Door	second Hicks
Nighness	second Hun
Heaven	Felt Jacket
Hive	third Hun
Brawler	second Door

Sentence(s):

The first **Shoe** was involved in the **Sequel** to the story, he stood at the **Gate** and gave a **Trite Epenthesis** for the word, "tax", to the first group of **Hicks**, at the **Cleft's Place** on the surface of the large rock, the first **Hun** has put the second **Shoe**, there was a **Clash** of the workers in the **Mine**, and he stood motionless under the **Tree** in a period of **Vacillation**.

He passed through the first **Door** and saw the second group of **Hicks**, whose **Nighness** to the second **Hun** was unexpected since they were not on good terms, he went to **Heaven** wearing the **Felt Jacket** and taking with him the **Hive**, and the third **Hun**, who was a **Brawler**, went through the second **Door**.

Example 20:   Password Length = 23 characters
Password: 6>9*7|08:63"25.34\7$6%8
Peg Words:

first Hicks	Grader Ban
Mine	Maverick
first Heaven	Surgical Garb
Hero	first Gate
Stolon	second Hicks
first Tree	Noble's Coat
Shoe	Hive
Rooftop	second Tree
Door	Backlash
second Heaven	Brawler
third Hicks	Descent
second Gate	

Sentence(s):

The first group of **Hicks** knew about the **Grader Ban** for road construction on the stretch of untarred road to the **Mine**, the **Maverick** went to **Heaven** wearing a **Surgical Garb**, the **Hero** went through the first **Gate** with the **Stolon** from the plant, and the second group of **Hicks** went to the first **Tree** and removed the **Noble's Coat** from it.

He found the **Shoe** placed in front of the **Hive** on the **Rooftop** quite close to the second **Tree**, he passed through the **Door** to witness the **Backlash** of protests from those who were refused entry into the second **Heaven**, and the **Brawler** confronted the third group of **Hicks** on the group's **Descent** down the slope to the second **Gate**.

Example 21: Password Length = 24 characters
Password: 3?1+8}67;26#18/50]49%3&2
Peg Words:

first Tree	Haitian Narc
first Hun	Truss
first Gate	Rat Race
first Hicks	Heaven
Mesocolon	first Shoe
second Hicks	Lumber
second Hun	second Gate
Clash	Hive
Hero	Bright Racquet
Door	Mine
Descent	second Tree
Undersigned	second Shoe

Sentence(s):

He reached the first **Tree** where the **Haitian Narc** was talking to the first **Hun**, he constructed the **Truss** near the first **Gate**, the **Rat Race** the first group of **Hicks** was involved in would not take them to **Heaven**, his **Mesocolon** was intact, and the first **Shoe** was taken by the second group of **Hicks** who had bought the **Lumber**.

The second **Hun** went through the second **Gate** to witness the **Clash** between the opposing groups of protesters, he took the **Hive** of the **Hero** together with the **Bright Racquet** and passed through the **Door**, and went to the **Mine**, after following the sharp **Descent** to the second **Tree**, and the one who **Undersigned** the lease took the second **Shoe**.

Example 22:   Password Length = 25 characters
Password: 0@8,33~01<71$75:64^51&3'6
Peg Words:

first Hero	Arcsine
Gate	Trauma
first Tree	second Tree
Hilde	second Hero
first Hun	Dress Van
first Heaven	second Hun
Brawler	second Heaven
first Hive	Stolon
first Hicks	Door
Carrot	second Hive
third Hun	Undersigned
third Tree	Singing Goat
second Hicks	

Sentence(s):

The first **Hero** found the **Arcsine** for the given angle, he passed through the **Gate** and suffered a **Trauma**, the first **Tree** and the second **Tree** were planted by **Hilde**, the second **Hero** took the first **Hun** to the **Dress Van** of the models, and when he left the first **Heaven**, he saw the second **Hun** and the **Brawler** in the second **Heaven**.

He took the first **Hive** and the **Stolon** from the plant and went into the garden belonging to the first group of **Hicks**, he went through the **Door** whilst chewing a **Carrot** and stood in front of the second **Hive**, the third **Hun** was the one who **Undersigned** the contract, and the shade of the third **Tree** was the resting place of the **Singing Goat** and the second group of **Hicks**.

5.4 Number-Special Character Practice Exercises

Exercises 1: Password Length = 4 characters

3!$0

4"%2

7#&6

6$'5

3%(8

9&)5

9'*6

1-+0

3.,4

0/4

Exercises 2: Password Length = 5 characters

7'3*4

6(0+0

6)7,0

8*8-0

4+1.5

0,3/5

4-7:5

9.0;3

4/7<9

1:2=7

Exercises 3: Password Length = 6 characters

6:8@=2

5;[0>7

0<6?\8

2=7@0

5]>6[7

3?3\^4

5@_]8
9`[8^2
3\4_{6
6]1`|5

Exercises 4:   Password Length = 7 characters
3]8`7}9
4^6{8~4
7_6|3!6
5`4}5"0
7{0~8#1
6|4!7$2
7}1"4%5
2~9#7&8
3|7$7'8
0"8%0(3

Exercises 5:   Password Length = 8 characters
1%90{8+2
8&9|5,34
9'67}4-5
2(6~3.94
0)28!4/6
4*9"78:2
4+76#0;1
9,0$63<1
9-62%4=8
8.2&9>57

Exercises 6:   Password Length = 9 characters
8>7[6^5{1
7?5\3_9|6

0@3]7`4}6
8[2^9{5~1
7\5_3|9!8
8]4`3}2"5
3^6{2~9#7
9_6|9!4$5
9`5}0"1%4
2{4~3#6&8

Exercises 7:   Password Length = 10 characters
3#5&2(41,6
7$1'8)2-30
2%4(8*53.0
9&3)5+4/52
0'6*7,45:1
6(5+4-1;37
8)0,1.530
9*8-2/04<5
8+4.1:0=79
8,9/3:17>6

Exercises 8:   Password Length = 11 characters
9?3\7_8}1"5
3@4]0`8~5#1
4[2^3{8!6$2
7\5_3|0"4%5
6]9`0}8#4&5
1^3{5~7$4'9
8_2|4!7%3(9
2`3}4"9&5)0
2{6~5#8'1*4
5|6!3$0(9+8

Exercises 9:   Password Length = 12 characters

7(8+0.9;52>7

1)5,6/27<6?0

4*8-9:14=3@6

4+3.9;75>1[4

5,8/9<01?6\7

0-8:6=49@6]3

8.7;5>28[3^5

4/9<7*6\34_2

8:4=9@3]61`5

4;0>5[68^1{3

Exercises 10:   Password Length = 13 characters

1{8~3#50&19)4

8|7!4$38'56*2

7}6"4%30(81+9

8~6#5&32)14,7

6!2$1'03*89-4

3"9%1(78+09.5

8#2&3)12,98/7

0$2'8*96-24:3

6%1(4+35.98;4

0&7)1,29/59<8

Exercises 11:   Password Length = 14 characters

9?8\1_3}67"0%9

3*5]2`7~1#64&7

8[9^6{3!75$0'6

6\0_5|2"74%9(8

8]3`5}4#67&8)0

5^6{2~1$43'9*5

5_3|4!8%67(4+9
8`3}6"7&25)4,1
0{3~9#2'56*7-9
6|8!1$2(09+7.5

Exercises 12:   Password Length = 15 characters
6.8;7>9[43^02{8
9/4<1?5\68_34|9
7:9=1@6]28`57}0
2;9>6[1^25{34~7
5<8?9\6_43|97!0
1=0@2]4`53}97"8
2>4[6^3{09~42#7
1?7\9_2|01*85$4
0@7]9`5}63"24%8
6[3^5{4~87#19&6

Exercises 13:   Password Length = 16 characters
2'7*1-84:6=8@2]2
9(2+3.02;4>5[1^0
7)0,3/49<4?5\7_9
3*8-9:18=5@7]8`2
2+1.8;67>5[1^9{6
8,2/5<81?8\5_7|1
6-8:8=49@2]8`0}5
7.1;9>54[9^1{3~3
9/4<0?89\0_4|7!8
5:2=0@52]3`0}6"0

Exercises 14:   Password Length = 17 characters
6"2%0(6+79,0;43>8
1#4&8)5,20-3<76?1

7$5'2*9-82.6=45@9
9%3(6+7.52/8>79[4
4&7)9,6/83:4?72\0
8'2*4-7:97;9@85]0
6(2+5.8:31<8[90^5
8)2,0/7<19=4\31_5
7*6-0:8=62>9]75{1
8+1.4;0>64?3^71|9

Exercises 15:   Password Length = 18 characters
6~7#2&9(73,46/86<5
8!3$1'2)07-96:58=7
2"9%0(2*46.04;61>5
1#7&6)5+34/91<50?7
9$5'0*6,74:86=09@3
6%9(1+8-73;02>01[5
3&8)4,2.05<63?08\9
3'2*9-1/46=91@03]6
8(5+0.6:19>42[87^0
3)7,6/2;74?50\68_0

Exercises 16:   Password Length = 19 characters
0!5$9'16*3-28:4=0@9
2"9%7(05+4.96;9>4[3
5#7&9)34,2/71<0?3\2
7$1'9*42-3:65=4@1]8
0%5(2+46.0;89>3[2^7
4&8)3,52/9<06?8\4_2
1'5*0-29:7=28@6]9`0
8(0+2.45;6>91[7^3{6
5)8,6/31<7?90\6_3|4
9*1-2:85=3@46]9`8}7

Exercises 17:   Password Length = 20 characters

4]7`3}79"12%8(09+5.1

5^3{8^64#92&5)17,8/3

9_2|6!20$60'8*76-9:3

2`6}2"97%30(8+95.6;0

6{1~7#80&43)0,27/4<7

1|6!0$87'19*6-83:1=4

8}7"2%41(05+6.29;2>3

2~4#9&67)83,5/41<8?0

1!7$2'62*95-3:40=8@1

6"4%7(80+50.1;86>7[9

Exercises 18:   Password Length = 21 characters

0;7>8[36^24{10~56#7&9

0<8?6\34_92|16!05$7'1

7=9@8]32`96}56"80%9(7

2>1[6^82{87~35#47&5)9

5?9\6_47|85!38$79`0*2

4@8]9`74}51"02%43(0+5

4[1^3{52~60#70&81)2,9

1\5_2|43!52$74`25*7-6

7]3`1}08"54%93(86+5.7

2^9{4~85#92&05)78,3/0

Exercises 19:   Password Length = 22 characters

1)9,5/84<23?74\16`52}0

3*9-0:76=41@87]21{05~8

8+2.5;61>09[85^74|90!3

2,7/8<36?04\98_15}42"0

0-3:4=08@72]81`06~57#4

3.5;6>40[98^13{52!67$0

0/8<9?62\03_27|94"85%1
0:6=4@90]54`87}23#89&7
5;7>1[94^93{78~02$82'4
1<4?3\90_28|64!72%05(3

Exercises 20:   Password Length = 23 characters
7"8%9(4+01.65;08>79[5^3
5#1&8)2,13/78<26?05\9_4
4$7'3*9-20:85=94@93]6`7
7%9(0+3.48;97>60[18^7{1
3&0)6,4/75<28?71\09_2|4
4'3*1-8:54=20@32]74`8}6
2(5+7.6;91>29[54^34{0~9
8)7,0/9<45?06\95_76|2!3
5*6-2:9=57@21]53`98}4"6
8+9.0;3>41[65^97{21~8#3

Exercises 21:   Password Length = 24 characters
1{2~1#80&45)03,78/69<1?2
0|7!8$45'06*79-12:94=3@0
3}5"0%16(94+06.27;98>6[0
3~6#5&27)91,62/45<09?8\1
8!0$9'12*73-41:52=67@4]8
6"3%2(87+54.17;23>20[9^8
7#2&6)54,83/10<67?48\5_9
3$0'9*56-74:08=13@92]1`8
5%8(6+71.98;10>34[65^7{8
1&3)5,70/89<24?84\65_3|7

Exercises 22:   Password Length = 25 characters
8\7_0|43!79$82'15*34-78:5
2]9`6}37"21%43(94+12.06;8
3^0{4~52#98&76)78,01/87<5

141

8_1|6!39$72'40*85-78:96=2
7`5}3"16%84(27+59.80;23>6
8{3~0#69&47)81,25/85<69?4
5|6!9$46'02*87-60:94=83@0
4}8"5%90(73+86.92;47>05[2
0~5#3&27)94,52/89<73?29\6
1!7$6'85*01-95:38=64@72]8

Numbers, Alphabets and Special Characters

Learning Procedure

1. You memorize the numbers, alphabets and special characters and their associated peg words. Memorize them very well through repetition and reinforcement because you will always have to remember them in order to recall the passwords.
2. You find the peg words for the numbers, alphabets and special characters in the password and arrange them in the order in which they appear in the password.
3. You construct sentences with the peg words in order to chain or link them sequentially and coherently together. The more outrageous a sentence is, the easier it is for you to remember it.
4. You memorize the sentences in order to get the correct positions of the peg words in the sentences with absolute ease.
5. You will then be able to remember the password if you remember the numbers, alphabets and special characters and their associated peg words.

How to Memorize the Sentences Constructed with the Peg Words

You will use repetition and reinforcement to learn these sentences.

1. Read the sentences inaudibly five or ten times.
2. Read the sentences audibly five or ten times.
3. Write down the sentences five or ten times.

Please continue this process till you can easily remember the sentences.

Please note that we have used the uppercase for initial letters of specific words or specific words in the groups of words in the sentences constructed in this book and bolded them only for emphasis and clarity. We crave your indulgence if you are unhappy that this may be an irremissible infraction of the rules of grammar.

5.5 Number-Alphabet-Special Character Examples

Example 1: Password Length = 4 characters
Password: 0A!3
Peg Words:

Hero	Hay
Vacillation	Tree

Sentence(s):
The **Hero** collected the **Hay** and without any **Vacillation** piled it under the **Tree**.

Example 2: Password Length = 5 characters
Password: 2a0"7
Peg Words:

Shoe   Little Hay

Hero   Noble's Coat

Heaven

Sentence(s):

He took the **Shoe** and a **Little Hay**, the **Hero** wore the **Noble's Coat** and went to **Heaven**.

Example 3:   Password Length = 6 characters

Password: 6B[#ℓ1

Peg Words:

Hicks   Bee

Felt Jacket   Lumber

Little Hell   Hun

Sentence(s):

The **Hicks** followed the **Bee** into the garden, he wore his **Felt Jacket** when hauling the **Lumber**, and it was a **Little Hell** for the **Hun**.

Example 4:   Password Length = 7 characters

Password: 1$b3M\8

Peg Words:

Hun   Brawler

Little Bee   Tree

Hem   Backlash

Gate

Sentence(s):

The **Hun** fought with the **Brawler**, the **Little Bee** buzzed around the **Tree**, the **Hem** of her dress was poorly sewn, and there was a great **Backlash** of protests at the **Gate** of his residence.

Example 5:   Password Length = 8 characters

Password: 3m6]7%C9

Peg Words:

Tree	Little Hem
Hicks	Bright Racquet
Heaven	Descent
Sea	Mine

Sentence(s):

She sat under the **Tree** and repaired the **Little Hem** of her daughter's dress, the **Hicks** bought a **Bright Racquet**, and he moved from **Heaven** in a slow **Descent** towards the **Sea** and ended up at the **Mine**.

Example 6:   Password Length = 9 characters
Password: 7&4N3^2c5
Peg Words:

Heaven	Undersigned
Door	Hen
Tree	Carrot
Shoe	Little Sea
Hive	

Sentence(s):

In **Heaven**, he **Undersigned** a contract to create a charity for the good of mankind, he opened the **Door** to the **Hen** coop, which was under the **Tree**, and he took a **Carrot**, wore the **Shoe** and went to the **Little Sea** whilst carrying the **Hive**.

Example 7:   Password Length = 10 characters
Password: 6'09n5D8_4
Peg Words:

Hicks	Singing Goat
Hero	Mine
Little Hen	Hive
Deal	Gate

Albacore	Door

Sentence(s):

The **Hicks** went with the **Singing Goat** to see the **Hero** in the **Mine**, the **Little Hen** was resting on the **Hive**, and he made a **Deal** at the **Gate** to export **Albacore** overseas, and then happily passed through the **Door** onto the street.

Example 8: Password Length = 11 characters
Password: 0`7(53d08Ө3
Peg Words:

first Hero	Singing Goat
Heaven	Best Epenthesis
Hive	first Tree
Little Deal	second Hero
Gate	Hole
second Tree	

Sentence(s):

The first **Hero** heard the **Singing Goat** singing in **Heaven**, he gave the **Best Epenthesis** for the word, "latch", he took the **Hive** and hung it on the first **Tree**, he had a **Little Deal** with the second **Hero** at the **Gate**, and he looked through the big **Hole** in the trunk of the second **Tree**.

Example 9: Password Length = 12 characters
Password: 1{9E7+W5)1o6
Peg Words:

first Hun	Cleft's Place
Mine	Eel
Heaven	Truss
Troubled Youth	Hive
Trite Epenthesis	second Hun
Little Hole	Hicks

Sentence(s):

The first **Hun** saw the **Cleft's Place** on the side of the mountain and went through to the **Mine**, he took the **Eel** to **Heaven**, the **Truss** was constructed by the **Troubled Youth**, he took the **Hive** and gave a **Trite Epenthesis** for the word, "mantis", to the second **Hun**, and looked through the **Little Hole** in the wall at the **Hicks** who were standing on the other side.

Example 10:   Password Length = 13 characters
Password: 9*2,5P14w7|e3
Peg Words:

Mine	Maverick
Shoe	Trauma
Hive	Pea
Hun	Door
Little Troubled Youth	Heaven
Surgical Garb	Little Eel
Tree	

Sentence(s):

The **Mine** was owned by the **Maverick** who was wearing a black **Shoe** and suffered a **Trauma** at the **Hive**, he took the **Pea** and gave it to the **Hun**, and passed through the **Door** to talk to the **Little Troubled Youth** who wanted to go to **Heaven**, and he was wearing the **Surgical Garb** when he took the **Little Eel** from the **Tree**.

Example 11:   Password Length = 14 characters
Password: 2-6p5}3+97F8X0
Peg Words:

Shoe	Nighness
Hicks	Little Pea
Hive	Rat Race

147

Tree	Truss
Mine	Heaven
Elf	Gate
Eggs	Hero

Sentence(s):

He wore the **Shoe** and wondered at the **Nighness** of the **Hicks** to the scene of the crime, he put the **Little Pea** on the **Hive**, he thought about the **Rat Race** going on in his life and then walked to the **Tree**, he looked at the **Truss** constructed at the opening of the **Mine**, he looked at **Heaven** and saw the **Elf** at the **Gate**, and he gave the **Eggs** to the **Hero**.

Example 12: Password Length = 15 characters
Password: 7x69~3f06,4Q6.8
Peg Words:

Heaven	Little Eggs
first Hicks	Mine
Hilde	Tree
Little Elf	Hero
second Hicks	Trauma
Door	Cue
third Hicks	Rooftop
Gate	

Sentence(s):

He went to **Heaven** with the **Little Eggs** he got from the first group of **Hicks** at the **Mine** owned by **Hilde**, the **Tree** was the refuge of the **Little Elf** whom the **Hero** reported to the second group of **Hicks** as having suffered a **Trauma**, he stood at the **Door** without having any **Cue** as to what the third group of **Hicks** was up to on the **Rooftop** close to the main **Gate**.

Example 13: Password Length = 16 characters
Password: 3!9Y8-4q0/2G5]d7
Peg Words:

Tree	Vacillation
Mine	Wile
Gate	Nighness
Door	Little Cue
Hero	Clash
Shoe	Gin
Hive	Bright Racquet
Little Deal	Heaven

Sentence(s):

He approached the **Tree**, showed some **Vacillation** before continuing to the **Mine**, fearing the **Wile** the gatekeeper was capable of utilizing to trick people at the **Gate**, he realized the **Nighness** of the **Door** to where he was standing, but did not have even a **Little Cue** as to what the **Hero** was planning to do there after the **Clash**, he wore the **Shoe**, drank a **Little Gin**, took the **Hive** and the **Bright Racquet**, made a **Little Deal** with his friends and went to **Heaven**.

Example 14: Password Length = 17 characters
Password: 4:2E3"0y1^9g8.4R5
Peg Words:

first Door	Stolon
Shoe	Eel
Tree	Noble's Coat
Hero	Little Wile
Hun	Carrot
Mine	Little Gin
Gate	Rooftop
second Door	Arc

Hive
Sentence(s):

He passed through the first **Door**, took the **Stolon** from the plant, the **Shoe** and the **Eel** and went to stand in the shade of the **Tree**, the **Noble's Coat** was worn by the **Hero**, the **Little Wile** employed by the **Hun** did not yield any results, he took the **Carrot** to the **Mine** after drinking a **Little Gin**, he went through the **Gate** and climbed to the **Rooftop**, he passed through the second **Door** and threw the ball in an **Arc** towards the **Hive**.

Example 15:   Password Length = 18 characters
Password: 58/1e3H4r6_9#5Z2;7
Peg Words:

first Hive	Gate
Clash	Hun
Little Eel	Tree
Age	Door
Little Arc	Hicks
Albacore	Mine
Lumber	second Hive
Zeal	Shoe
Mesocolon	Heaven

Sentence(s):

He took the first **Hive** and passed through the **Gate**, he was involved in a **Clash** with the **Hun**, he took the **Little Eel** to the **Tree** whose **Age** was unknown, he opened the **Door** and saw the **Little Arc** drawn by the **Hicks** on the wall, he grilled the **Albacore** and took it to the **Mine**, the **Lumber** was moved to the shed where the second **Hive** was, with **Zeal** he took the **Shoe** and entered the room, and he realized that there was a problem with his **Mesocolon** before going to **Heaven**.

Example 16: Password Length = 19 characters

Password: 4z5`9$60F5S<8h17:02

Peg Words:

Door	Little Zeal
first Hive	Brave Ascent
Mine	Brawler
Hicks	first Hero
Elf	second Hive
Hearse	Dress Van
Gate	Little Age
Hun	Heaven
Stolon	second Hero
Shoe	

Sentence(s):

He passed through the **Door** with **Little Zeal,** carrying the first **Hive** and made the **Brave Ascent** to the **Mine** on the mountain side, the **Brawler** fought with the **Hicks,** the first **Hero** saw the **Elf** carrying the second **Hive** to the **Hearse,** the **Dress Van** of the mannequins was at the main **Gate** of the fairgrounds, the **Little Age** of the **Hun** could not be compared with that of **Heaven,** and he gave the **Stolon** from the plant to the second **Hero** who had the **Shoe.**

Example 17: Password Length = 20 characters

Password: 7%3s0#J8f6{4;5l6A2=1

Peg Words:

Heaven	Descent
Tree	Little Hearse
Hero	Lumber
Jay	Gate
Little Elf	first Hicks
Cleft's Place	Door

Mesocolon	Hive
Eye	second Hicks
Hay	Shoe
Sequel	Hun

Sentence(s):

From **Heaven**, he followed his **Descent** to the **Tree** where the **Little Hearse** that was carrying the mortal remains of the **Hero** was parked, he saw the **Lumber** on the field and the **Jay** flying about in the air above it, he passed through the **Gate** and saw the **Little Elf** and the first group of **Hicks** heading towards the **Cleft's Place** on the hillside, he opened the **Door** and complained about his **Mesocolon**, he took the **Hive** and with an **Eye** on the second group of **Hicks**, he continued to where the **Hay** was, he wore the **Shoe** and went to the cinema to watch the **Sequel** of the story about the **Hun**.

Example 18:   Password Length = 21 characters
Password: 6G8a1&3~2|9i8$7T2j1<4
Peg Words:

Hicks	Gin
first Gate	Little Hay
first Hun	Undersigned
Tree	Hilde
first Shoe	Surgical Garb
Mine	Little Eye
second Gate	Brawler
Heaven	Tea
second Shoe	Little Jay
second Hun	Dress Van
Door	

Sentence(s):

The **Hicks** drank some **Gin**, passed through the first **Gate**, took a **Little Hay** for the sheep of the first **Hun**, who **Undersigned** the contract under the **Tree** with **Hilde**, who was wearing the first **Shoe** and the **Surgical Garb**, and had the intention of going to the **Mine**.

He looked through the **Little Eye** of the needle at the second **Gate** where the **Brawler** was negotiating to enter **Heaven**, and he had some **Tea** before wearing the second **Shoe** and looking at the **Little Jay** circling over the head of the second **Hun**, who was standing near the **Dress Van** whose **Door** was painted pink.

Example 19: Password Length = 22 characters
Password: 8=3%B'15}2J6g79K35t8?6
Peg Words:

first Gate	Sequel
first Tree	Descent
Bee	Singing Goat
Hun	first Hive
Rat Race	Shoe
Jay	first Hicks
Little Gin	Heaven
Mine	Quay
second Tree	second Hive
Little Tea	second Gate
Haitian Narc	second Hicks

Sentence(s):

The first **Gate** featured in the **Sequel** of his story involving the first **Tree** and his **Descent** into the quagmire, the **Bee** buzzed around the head of the **Singing Goat** whilst the **Hun** was carrying the first **Hive** to the garden, he thought about the **Rat Race** he was involved in, he wore his **Shoe** and saw the **Jay** flying about in front of the house of the first group of **Hicks**.

He drank a **Little Gin** and attempted to go to **Heaven**, he came out of the **Mine** and went to the **Quay**, on the second **Tree** you would find the second **Hive**, and he drank a **Little Tea**, passed through the second **Gate**, and saw the **Haitian Narc** interrogating the second group of **Hicks**.

Example 20: Password Length = 23 characters
Password: 36>8H4~9U2(5b4&8j14k2@5
Peg Words:

Tree	Hicks
Grader Ban	first Gate
Age	first Door
Hilde	Mine
New	first Shoe
Best Epenthesis	first Hive
Little Bee	second Door
Undersigned	second Gate
Little Jay	Hun
third Door	Little Quay
second Shoe	Arcsine
second Hive	

Sentence(s):

The **Tree** was planted by the **Hicks**, there was a **Grader Ban** for road construction from the first **Gate** to about a kilometer away, he knew her **Age** before passing through the first **Door** and meeting **Hilde**, he drove from the **Mine** in his **New** car, wearing the first **Shoe**, and he gave the **Best Epenthesis** for the word, "grass", and took the **Hive** to the field with the **Little Bee** circling around it.

He passed through the second **Door**, and **Undersigned** the contract, and then passed through the second **Gate**, the **Little Jay** flew over the head of the **Hun** as he stood in the garden, he went through the third **Door** and went to the **Little Quay**, wearing the second **Shoe**, and he found the **Arcsine** of the angle before coming to the second **Hive**.

Example 21: Password Length = 24 characters
Password: 5!0C#4[0L1u7)8M6%5h3K?09
Peg Words:

first Hive	Vacillation
first Hero	Sea
Lumber	Door
Felt Jacket	second Hero
Hell	Hun
Little New	Heaven
Trite Epenthesis	Gate
Hem	Hicks
Descent	second Hive
Little Age	Tree
Quay	Haitian Narc
third Hero	Mine

Sentence(s):

He took the first **Hive**, showed some **Vacillation** before going to meet the first **Hero** at **Sea**, the **Lumber** was packed close to the **Door**, he wore the **Felt Jacket** of the second **Hero** and went to **Hell**, and the **Hun** was wearing a **Little New** shirt which he took to **Heaven**.

He gave a **Trite Epenthesis** for the word, "patch", before passing through the **Gate**, he had the **Hem** of his daughter's dress repaired before he met the **Hicks** for a discussion, he watched their **Descent** downhill to the second **Hive**, he was surprised by the **Little Age** of the giant **Tree**, and on the **Quay** stood the **Haitian Narc**, talking to the third **Hero**, who owned the **Mine**.

Example 22:   Password Length = 25 characters
Password: 2$9@4I5"0℮5V4*4k9\7&9c1m3
Peg Words:

Shoe	Brawler
first Mine	Arcsine
first Door	Eye
first Hive	Noble's Coat
Hero	Little Hell
second Hive	Veal
second Door	Maverick
third Door	Little Quay
second Mine	Backlash
Heaven	Undersigned
third Mine	Little Sea
Hun	Little Hem
Tree	

Sentence(s):

The **Shoe** of the **Brawler** was shiny, he went to the first **Mine** and determined the **Arcsine** of the angle, he passed through the first **Door**, with an **Eye** on how he would benefit from the first **Hive** which was loaned to him, he saw the **Noble's Coat** worn by the **Hero** before escaping from the **Little Hell**, he took the second **Hive**, and ate some **Veal**.

He went through the second **Door** and saw the **Maverick**, entering the third **Door**, before going to the **Little Quay** where the boat was, he went to the second **Mine** amid the **Backlash** of protests due to the accident, he went to **Heaven** and **Undersigned** a contract to do good to humanity, the third **Mine** was close to the **Little Sea**, and the **Hun** had the **Little Hem** of his daughter's dress mended under the **Tree**.

5.6 Number-Alphabet-Special Character Practice Exercises

Exercises 1:   Password Length = 4 characters
0#b1
8C$0
6c%6
6&D3
7'd2
2(E5
5e)2
2*F3
8+f4
1,G5

Exercises 2:   Password Length = 5 characters
8E9&6
0'2e4
5(8F1
4f6)7
3G7*6
4+5g0
2H9,5
95h-3
7I6.8
1/2i5

Exercises 3:   Password Length = 6 characters
9h)K,2
0k-l*6
7.iL+0

6,ℓ/J3
3j-M:7
0.K;m5
2<N/k1
7L:=n3
10>ℓ;6
5<Mo?1

Exercises 4:   Password Length = 7 characters
1N<6/q7
3R=4n:5
9r;O8>2
5S?6<o9
2@P=9s0
1T[0p>8
4\Q?6t5
7U]2@q3
9^R[1u3
5V_7r\8

Exercises 5:   Password Length = 8 characters
2t5W1?\2
7@4]U5w3
0u2^X6[8
9x7\0_V8
2v3`Y0]5
3^4y7{W6
2w6|Z5_8
0z}4`9X7
6x{1~9A2
9a!8|7Y6

Exercises 6:   Password Length = 9 characters

2Z8_3c0|9

3`7D5}8z2

3~1A5{7d6

5a7E9!8|6

7"9e4}8B3

1F5^3b0#4

7C6$4f3!0

1G2"7%9c8

9D1&3g2#8

8&3H'64d5

Exercises 7:   Password Length = 10 characters

8f75I2$6!2

6i2%3"7G94

63#8g4&7J2

9H30$4j9'8

5(0K7%68h2

6&30I2k4)5

7i51'3L8*7

84ℓ9+6J5(0

0)7j94M2,8

6m89*3-K12

Exercises 8:   Password Length = 11 characters

2L'36o52*41

98+7P5(9I46

5)6M70p1,48

3Q6-4*78m05

0+7N2.31q68

6R04/71n8,4

7:4⊕6-8r241

431.S62;8o4
2P0<47/98s3
03T5:8p9=72

Exercises 9:   Password Length = 12 characters
8r9=4x0:U-26
47u8.5>S1Y;3
0<3s6y4V8/?9
0Z@2:5v6=3T4
8;3>2t6z[7W5
3U4\7w3<8?A5
7@9X6a=8u3]0
0^6V9>4x8B[1
9Y6?1\b7_0v2
6W3]8y9@C2`5

Exercises 10:   Password Length = 13 characters
2A85@4]6d`7G9
12g6E{5a3[4^7
4e0_1B7\2H8|6
61h7]5`9}F8b3
76C0{3I~8^2f4
4_3G6i5c|0!82
2D1"5`8g7}9J6
21H~8j3d#7{04
1K0$7E!6|59h8
75I6}8"k3%1e2

Exercises 11:   Password Length = 14 characters
4j1%3}5M26p8"7
0#6Q7m3~0K8&45
5'3!4k7$6q9N83

5n67R4(2"3%L16

76l4&2#8O9r5)0

7S5*1o3'0M8$62

2m0%95s8(6+4P3

9)73p4,5&2T7N8

2t87n6*9Q5'2-4

30q4(1.6U8O7+5

Exercises 12:   Password Length = 15 characters

5S7(18+46v9Y3.1

41y26W4/5s0,9)8

47*5-8T3Z2w41:5

10X7z2;6+3.49t8

02U6,8x04A7<3/9

08:79a2=5u0-3Y8

38.5>1V4;0y9B67

8v9<7bZ5?43/216

9@6:04=87WC50z9

1A7c4w2[8;53>15

Exercises 13:   Password Length = 16 characters

9b8[7H^4>5E3k2;6

4\1e2<4C_3L9?7h8

7`2c8lℓ9]6@2F3=4

1i7f6^M{8>02D9[4

9?8m7|d0\4J5_G60

5}E3j4]9g8@7N`06

8[5H1n~6{3K9^1e7

0k6O9\8F_3!4h5|2

7f3`5}L10"l8o6]4

24i5^3#P~9{8ℓ9G1

161

Exercises 14:   Password Length = 17 characters

2N#07w2&3q8T1{6~0
1$7!9R3t2|8n'5X10
9x8U3}1Ө2(5"7r4%0
1)8S7#6&1Y9~3o1u0
8P15!2V1$*3s6y4'7
6v9%4(T7Z0"5+1p38
3#9Q1z2,4&)8t5W60
1U7'5*2w6$-9q1A82
3.2X7%6a0(24u5R+8
6r97V5,B8x3&6/2)4

Exercises 15:   Password Length = 18 characters

5z9)6,0<3f9I04/1C2
9i36c7:2-8A6*5G3=4
8+0a3>6g9J5.3D4;26
9j8/04d5<7,3?2H1B0
0h3=06-9b8:7E@2K43
75C6[I0e3k1>9.87;2
1F0?5L8/6<71c9\0i1
6@7]9J3=8D2:5I40f1
4;9^62M0[3G8j6>5d4
7K1<6?5_E4\3m28g09

Exercises 16:   Password Length = 19 characters

0L518u4R2?3\9o4_6|7
16@5P7`0V6}3Ɩ24]9r8
62M7~5p[1^S09v8{207
5Q48s2|7!9W13_8\4m0
06`0w}7]8N9"6T43q15
4n75#R8t2{3^09X8~73
8|23U6x170!8r9$Ө5_4

9`8S0"7o4%06Y1}38u1
62&4V7~13{6#8s9P5y2
9!0p32T6Z48v5'2|7$6

Exercises 17:   Password Length = 20 characters
2x3*7d_5G'4$6A8!69j1
2+5g1(3a6"7K8Y0%4E`9
0k49{5y2&8e7H)6B#3,0
1$5'F-8*7h3b|6L49Z12
8(9+0z2ℓ45f6%7l5.C}3
7~3c8&5i97)4A6,G0M/8
9a4!8g1m-3D2'9:0J5*6
24j36(9;B+8d5H2.N7"4
3b8n9#E0/6h28)6<K4,3
10-6k$2θ4l=7C8e0:9*5

Exercises 18:   Password Length = 21 characters
2M4=9S7'6Y8@2v9]5p2:3
8^04Q6[7W>9;2m3y5(9s8
73w0)N_8?6T5o26q4<1Z\9
4@5]9t2=6z9*R1`03X7n8
62θ5r8x9^4A{3>7[02+U6
0Sa98u25?0,6\Y3_9o7|4
7y4`5s6]2P9B@8-9V3}17
8{9p0[9v5~0.7T1^3Z2b5
0t6!7W2_1z/3C9|6Q8\54
3q5:74c0}2U6]8`A"9w07

Exercises 19:   Password Length = 22 characters
8b7-6@9K4:0h5*7=3E0n62
5;9θ48>16e0[8k7C9l+2.3
0F18,3i0L9c4<2/8o6?5\7

1=7D24P:3@1]5I6f8-4J09
9[4M1.0G5^2>8j7;2p3d16
7Q9?0<4K8E6m5/3\20_1g8
3`H9]4N2:9@0=13k71q9e2
7^45L8R97F{6n90>3h[2;1
4<7|2f5\6Ꞛ7_8I9?3ɭ58r2
3i9@5}4S16M7G2]8o5=9`7

Exercises 20: Password Length = 23 characters
9Q8`3W1}7C5%62z40t5]8"6
95A8~2U4#71w0^9c6q5&0{7
3u5|0'D6_8X4R2!04a17$35
03r4%9B27}6"4(8V6`9x2d3
6~9)2E8{70S1&9Y3b42v8$0
18%3W14y29!0e2|6*C7'5s4
2F2}8T9+6c7(3w84"27&1Z5
06)4X1#7z03f2'1t84D,5~9
7-9G26!3d84$1*5x07A8(U3
1a7%3)0u1+8"20g5.9E3Y46

Exercises 21: Password Length = 24 characters
0f247o1>3u8(7.5L[0R;X1+9
3\6V7)4,5ℓ1<6x9r8?G/3P27
8:0p9S@1]2v5*3g4-0M5Y6=1
7m5H9.4y0>3s[8Q6+2W1^2;4
34,6T2q\7<9N1_4w5?Z6/3h8
5z3X8`6-I7:2R]9@0t1=4n53
5>6Ꞛ4;9^U[0{7A3x1.28i7r0
3|2a8J7/0X1?8Y<6o9\2u3_5
9`P3V]7@8=52j1}8:B54x9y6
6Y5;Z~8{b9p16>0^7v3[5K24

Exercises 22:   Password Length = 25 characters

5A3^1#6M!2p4d1G9~02j8$2{7
4%3K6!2E5`9|6a7Q1$8m4"0g7
6q24}1$5&H8%2k9N7e6{3B8"0
3F16&27b9R|8~0h5$1L9'2%n4
1%9&6(I5I0}9f7!308C493r82
8c37o4'8M9(2S4&7~G0"5i6)9
95'4g6!3s2$7J(1*5P9{2D7m8
5+7N0%8d9p|16^3H2"9T8*2j0
1Q8$}3+4t70h2K5&9n6+8)3E1
2k3*804'51e2,7%6q8-U~9I05

Conclusion

I hope you have realized how simple it is to utilize these techniques. I highly recommend the use of the character rhyme peg systems which are based on rhymes and near-rhymes of the characters. The beauty of the character rhyme peg system is that you can reasonably guess which characters the rhymes or near-rhymes are referring to.

These mnemonic techniques will definitely help you to memorize both simple and complex passwords. The best password length is a moot point. Some accounts may prescribe minimum and maximum permissible numbers of characters. Some systems like the Automatic Teller Machine (ATM) require a four (4) digit password. I will however recommend that in situations where there are no such restrictions, you use a minimum of ten characters and a maximum of twenty characters, although these memorization techniques can be used for any length of password, even for a length of two hundred and fifty-six characters, if necessary.

As you can see you have to invest time and energy to memorize the passwords but it is clearly worthwhile. You should not be discouraged if you are having some difficulty in memorizing. It is always difficult to increase your performance in any endeavor so you should be ready to do your utmost to achieve your goals.

www.ingramcontent.com/pod-product-compliance
Lightning Source LLC
Chambersburg PA
CBHW071128050326
40690CB00008B/1381